CAMPAIGN • 203

TRENTON AND PRINCETON 1776–77

Washington crosses the Delaware

DAVID BONK

ILLUSTRATED BY GRAHAM TURNER

Series editors Marcus Cowper and Nikolai Bogdanovic

First published in Great Britain in 2009 by Osprey Publishing,
Midland House, West Way, Botley, Oxford OX2 0PH, UK
443 Park Avenue South, New York, NY 10016, USA
E-mail: info@ospreypublishing.com

A CIP catalog record for this book is available from the British Library

Print ISBN: 978 1 84603 350 6
PDF e-book ISBN: 978 1 84603 821 1

Editorial by Ilios Publishing Ltd, Oxford, UK (www.iliospublishing.com)
Page layout by The Black Spot
Index by Michael Forder
Typeset in Sabon and Myriad Pro
Maps by Bounford.com
3D bird's-eye views by The Black Spot
Battlescene illustrations by Graham Turner
Originated by PPS Grasmere Ltd., Leeds
Printed in China through Worldprint Ltd.

09 10 11 12 13   10 9 8 7 6 5 4 3 2 1

FOR A CATALOG OF ALL BOOKS PUBLISHED BY OSPREY MILITARY AND
AVIATION PLEASE CONTACT:

NORTH AMERICA
Osprey Direct, c/o Random House Distribution Center, 400 Hahn Road,
Westminster, MD 21157
E-mail: uscustomerservice@ospreypublishing.com

ALL OTHER REGIONS
Osprey Direct, The Book Service Ltd, Distribution Centre, Colchester Road,
Frating Green, Colchester, Essex, CO7 7DW
E-mail: customerservice@ospreypublishing.com

www.ospreypublishing.com

Osprey Publishing are supporting the Woodland Trust, the UK's leading
woodland conservation charity, by funding the dedication of trees.

ACKNOWLEDGMENTS

To Eugene Bonk, Joseph Bonk, Stanley Bonk and Edwin Bonk, who,
like Washington's army of 1776, answered the call to arms during their
country's hour of peril.

PICTURE CREDITS

Unless otherwise noted illustrations are from the United States
National Archives.

ARTIST'S NOTE

Readers may care to note that the original paintings from which the
colour plates in this book were prepared are available for private sale.
All reproduction copyright whatsoever is retained by the Publishers.
All enquiries should be addressed to:

Graham Turner
PO Box 568
Aylesbury
Buckinghamshire
HP17 8ZK
UK

www.studio88.co.uk

The Publishers regret that they can enter into no correspondence
upon this matter.

Key to military symbols

CONTENTS

ORIGINS OF THE CAMPAIGN

With the fall of Fort Washington on November 16, 1776, the cause of American independence appeared to teeter on the brink of failure. American fortunes never seemed brighter than after the British evacuation of Boston in March 1776. Although there was jubilation at the British retreat American commander-in-chief General George Washington knew the British would be back. Even as the British were preparing to sail from Boston Washington had ordered men and *matériel* shifted south to New York. As early as January Washington had dispatched Major-General Charles Lee to assume command of the city and prepare its defenses.

The heady days of spring quickly turned sullen in June 1776 when the British fleet arrived off New York and General William Howe's British Army established themselves on Long Island. As summer turned to fall Washington and his army suffered a series of demoralizing defeats. While the Americans avoided catastrophic defeat, Washington was outmaneuvered and outgeneraled and his army was driven out of New York. Unsure of Howe's intentions Washington consulted his senior officers and decided on November 6, 1776, to divide the army into four distinct commands. The largest force, 7,000 men under Maj. Gen. Charles Lee, was assigned the task of blocking any British move north into New England. Major-General William Heath was given 4,000 men and assigned the objective of defending the Hudson Highlands at Peekskill, New York. Washington retained about 2,000 men to defend New Jersey and to support Major-General Nathaniel Greene, who was given command of the strategic forts Washington and Lee along the Hudson River.

The Americans began their movements on November 7 and Washington left White Plains on November 10, reaching Fort Lee to confer with Major-General Greene on November 13. To defend the two forts Greene had over 5,000 men under his command. Greene assured Washington that Fort Washington could hold out for several days and if forced to retreat the garrison could safely cross the Hudson River. Although Washington had recognized the vulnerability of Fort Washington and been disposed to abandon it, Maj. Gen. Greene had convinced him that its defenses were strong enough to delay the British long enough to allow for an orderly withdrawal. Against his own judgment Washington accepted Greene's argument.

The British attack on Fort Washington began early on November 16 and by 4.00pm over 2,800 American defenders had surrendered. General Washington watched helplessly in growing despair and disillusionment from across the Hudson River at Fort Lee.

"The Spirit of 76" This 19th-century illustration is an idealized view of the citizen soldiers who sustained the American Army through the dark period of Washington's retreat through New Jersey.

Although Washington took no action against Greene, who had shown organizational talents in arguing for the establishment of a series of supply points across New Jersey in the event of a retreat, his confidence had been shaken. Washington noted that Maj. Gen. Greene had erred in his judgment in believing Fort Washington could be defended. Confidence in Washington's leadership had already begun to erode as the American Army was pushed out of New York. The loss of Fort Washington gave further evidence to his critics that Howe had outgeneraled him.

With the losses in manpower from the battles around New York, the recent surrender of over 2,800 at Fort Washington and the deployment of another 2,000 men at Fort Lee, Washington was left with the poorly trained and equipped units of the Flying Camp. These were militia units raised by Congress in June 1776 from Maryland, Delaware and Pennsylvania intended to act as a mobile reserve and defend New Jersey from invasion. Their enlistments were scheduled to expire on December 1 or December 30. They included Brigadier-General Nathaniel Heard's New Jersey Militia, Brigadier-General Reazin Beall's New Jersey Militia and Pennsylvania Militia under the command of Brigadier-General James Ewing.

Washington realized the loss of Fort Washington rendered Fort Lee untenable to defend and dangerous for the troops garrisoned there. He ordered Greene to begin the process of withdrawing the defenders and the large quantity of supplies to the relative safety of the interior of New Jersey. Greene wrote to Washington on November 18 that he had begun to remove the supplies. Greene reported that he did not trust the powder and ammunition to water transport and was struggling to find enough wagons to carry away the supplies. Given Gen. Howe's ponderous style of pursuit the slow pace of the removal of supplies did not appear to raise serious concerns.

Late on the night of November 19 British and Hessian troops under Lieutenant-General Charles Earl Cornwallis crossed the Hudson River several miles north of the fort at Lower Cloister Landing, New Jersey, and under cover of a cold rain and damp mist climbed the Palisades, a range of steep bluffs along the Hudson. American patrols had been stationed along the Palisades but the Lower Cloister Landing, at the foot of the Palisades, was considered an unlikely crossing point.

The British and Hessian troops climbed a narrow four-foot path to the crest, dragging their artillery behind. Cornwallis's taskforce, numbering 5,000 men, included British light infantry and Hessian *Jäger*, British and Hessian grenadiers, British guards, Highlanders of the Black Watch, the British 33rd Regiment and the Queen's American Rangers. The combined British and Hessian troops, arriving in two waves, began disembarking at 8.00am and by 10.00am the entire force was ashore. By the time the infantry climbed the narrow path and the artillery was manhandled to the top of the bluff it was after 1.00pm. Although Fort Lee lay only five-and-a-half miles directly to the south the distance by road was closer to 10 miles and the main British force did not begin its march until mid-afternoon.

Washington received word of the British attack at 10.00am at his headquarters in the Zabriskie Mansion at Hackensack, New Jersey, five miles from Fort Lee. Washington sent orders to Maj. Gen. Nathaniel Greene, commanding the Fort Lee garrison, to retreat immediately and then directed American troops to secure the village crossroads at Liberty Pole and the New Bridge across the Hackensack River. New Bridge was approximately

four miles north of Hackensack and about seven miles from Fort Lee. The Liberty Pole crossroads was located between New Bridge and the fort.

Washington and several aides crossed the Hackensack River and rode to meet the retreating garrison. Washington, still concerned about a possible British move toward Liberty Pole, only two miles from the British assembly point, decided to remain at the crossroads and wait for the retreating garrison. Possession of both Liberty Pole and New Bridge were critical to covering the retreat of the Fort Lee troops. If the British captured either position they would cut off the retreat of the Fort Lee garrison. Washington also ordered one aide to return to Hackensack and send an immediate note to Maj. Gen. Lee, detailing the rapidly developing situation and directing him to cross the Hudson River according to previously agreed plans. The message noted that detachments of the enemy were only two miles north of Liberty Pole.

Greene, alerted at approximately the same time as Washington that the British had landed, ordered an evacuation. Rather than immediately quit the fort the garrison inexplicably settled down for breakfast. Only later did the garrison begin a haphazard retreat. It was six miles from the fort to the relative safety of New Bridge. The disordered column moved slowly to Liberty Pole, where Washington and his aides accompanied them across New Bridge to Hackensack. Greene, returning to Fort Lee, rounded up several hundred laggards but left 100–200 mostly drunk stragglers to be taken prisoner by the British.

British light infantry and Hessian *Jäger* had first secured the bluffs and then fanned out far ahead of the main force. Captain Ewald led his Hessian *Jäger* toward the New Bridge crossing of the Hackensack River and engaged part of the retreating American Army. Recognizing the opportunity to cut off some of the retreating Americans, Ewald requested reinforcements from Cornwallis. To his surprise Cornwallis refused his request and ordered him to break off

Washington and Staff at Fort Lee, Watching the Battle of Fort Washington John Ward Dunsmore. Washington and Maj. Gen. Nathaniel Greene watched the British and Hessian assault on Fort Washington from across the Hudson River at Fort Lee. Rather than resisting the British assault as Greene had promised Washington watched in dismay as the fort surrendered. (Fraunces Tavern Museum/Sons of the Revolution in State of New York. Gift of George A. Zabriske Memorial, 1936. 2006 Conservation sponsored by the Bayand Paul Foundation)

contact with the enemy. Cornwallis chided Ewald, "Let them go my dear Ewald, and stay here. We do not want to lose any men. One *Jäger* is worth more than ten rebels." Cornwallis' reaction suggests he was clearly more intent on capturing Fort Lee than on running down the enemy army. Cornwallis could not be entirely certain that the Americans were in wholesale retreat and may have suspected that despite the movement of some disorganized elements the main American force might elect to make a stand as they did at Fort Washington. He also knew that the removal of supplies and heavy ordnance required time and investing Fort Lee should be the first objective.

At dusk the main British force entered Fort Lee, capturing 18 pieces of artillery, tents, food and most of the American entrenching tools. The British also took several thousand head of cattle. British patrols advanced to the Hackensack River while the main force settled down in Fort Lee. Meanwhile the Americans continued their flight into New Jersey. A Hackensack resident described the retreat: "The night was dark, cold and rainy, but I had a fair view of Greene's troops from the light of the windows as they passed on our side of the street. They marched two abreast, looked ragged, some without a shoe on their feet and most of them wrapped in their blankets."

CHRONOLOGY

1776

October 28 Battle of White Plains.

October 31/ November 1 Washington retires across Bronx River.

November 4 British Army retires toward King's Bridge, New York.

November 7 After a council of war Washington divides American Army into four parts.

November 10 Washington retires into New Jersey and directs Maj. Gen. Lee to be ready to support him if the British invade New Jersey.

November 16 British and Hessian forces capture Fort Washington.

November 20 Lieutenant-General Cornwallis crosses Hudson River and Greene evacuates Fort Lee. American Army retreats to Hackensack.

November 21 Washington requests Lee march to his assistance.

November 22 Americans retreat from Hackensack to Newark. British, under Lt. Gen. Cornwallis, pursue.

November 24 Congress authorizes Washington to request reinforcements from Northern Department. Washington receives Lee's reply explaining his delay.

November 26 Cornwallis advances toward Newark.

November 27 Washington demands Lee immediately march to join his army.

November 28 Washington sends sick to Morristown and retires to Brunswick.

November 29 Americans occupy New Brunswick and British march from Newark.

December 1 British engage American forces at New Brunswick. Washington orders all boats along Delaware River collected.

December 2 British occupy New Brunswick as Americans retreat to Trenton. Seven regiments from Northern Department are dispatched to Washington. Lee begins movement toward Washington.

December 7 British advance from New Brunswick to Princeton. American Army begins crossing Delaware River.

December 10 Washington rejects Lee's proposal to remain on the British flank and affirms his order to join the main army.

December 12 Lee orders his force to join Washington. Colonel Rall occupies Trenton with two Hessian regiments.

December 13 Lee is captured at Basking Ridge tavern. Howe suspends his pursuit and issues orders for winter quarters.

December 14	Washington suggests possible attack on British in New Jersey.
December 19	Thomas Paine publishes *The American Crisis*.
December 20	Lee's force arrives at Washington's camp.
December 23	Donop advances against American militia at Mt. Holly.
December 24	Rall receives warning from Major-General Grant that Americans are planning an attack. Washington holds council of war to finalize details of attack.
December 25/26	Battle of Trenton.
December 27	Cadwalader and militia cross the Delaware River.
December 28	Donop, alerted to Cadwalader's crossing, marches to Princeton.
December 29	Washington directs his army to re-cross the Delaware. Cadwalader marches to Bordentown.
December 30	Crossing of American units completed. Enlistments begin to expire and most Continental units resolve to leave. Washington convenes council of war in Trenton to review options.

1777

January 1	Grant marches to Princeton where Cornwallis joins him.
January 2	Cadwalader arrives in Trenton. Cornwallis begins his advance to Trenton. British and Hessian troops push Americans through Trenton but fail to cross Assunpink Creek. Washington resolves to move against Princeton.
January 3	Battle of Princeton.
January 4	Washington marches to Boundbrook. Cornwallis marches to New Brunswick.
January 7	Washington marches to Morristown.

OPPOSING COMMANDERS

General George Washington. He is shown here as a militia colonel during the French and Indian War. Washington served as commander of the Virginia Militia and aide to General Braddock.

AMERICAN

George Washington (1732–99). A veteran of the French and Indian War, serving as lieutenant-colonel of Virginia Militia and aide to General Braddock, Washington had extensive military experience by the time of his appointment as American commander-in-chief in 1775. In 1755 Washington and several companies of militia had defeated a force of French and Indians at Great Meadows, only to surrender Fort Necessity five weeks later. As aide to Braddock Washington suffered through the battle of the Wilderness in July 1755, in which Braddock was fatally wounded and the British Army routed along the Monongahela River. During the battle Washington escaped unscathed despite exposing himself to enemy fire and having several horses killed under him. An Indian chief later declared that Washington was under the protection of the Great Spirit and as a favorite of Heaven he would never die in battle. In 1758 Washington, now in command of all Virginia Militia, assisted the British in capturing Fort Duquesne and then retired from military service. At the beginning of the Revolution, Washington was a wealthy planter and landowner in Virginia, serving in the Virginia House of Burgesses and as a representative to the First Continental Congress. Washington was appointed commander-in-chief in an effort to solidify support from southern states for the armed struggle.

By the time of the Trenton and Princeton campaign Washington had been tested by fire, leading the army through the heady days of the capture of Boston, the frustrations of the defeats around New York, the humiliation of the loss of Fort Washington and the despair of the retreat across New Jersey. The Trenton and Princeton campaign was the first real glimpse of genius in Washington's military judgment. Although he was to suffer a series of reverses throughout the later years of the Revolution his audacious strike at Trenton, his management of the defense of the Assunpink Creek and his personal intervention to rally the army at Princeton showed him as a superior military strategist and tactician.

Charles Lee (1731–82). Lee was born in England and accompanied his father's regiment, the 44th Foot, to America in 1754. A veteran of the fight along the Monongahela, Lee was adopted by the Mohawks and married a chief's daughter. He fought and was wounded at Ticonderoga in 1758 and returned to England. He served under John Burgoyne in Portugal in 1762 before taking service as an aide to King Stanislaus of Poland. Rising to the rank of major-general he fought the Turks with the Russians before returning

to England and being promoted to lieutenant-colonel in 1772. With no prospects for assignment he resigned his commission and emigrated to America in 1773. Lee joined the American Army in 1775 and served at Boston. He was sent by Washington to supervise the construction of defenses around New York and then sent to take command of the Southern Department in March 1776. He organized the defense of Charleston in June and was recalled to New York where he fought at White Plains.

Lee's role in the retreat from New York diminishes his obvious military talent. His reluctance to join Washington promptly after the fall of Fort Lee reflected his lack of confidence in Washington's military judgment. Ironically, Lee's actions, which seemed to worry Cornwallis and Howe, contributed to the slow British advance and gave Washington the time needed to retreat into Pennsylvania. While Lee's justification for remaining at Peekskill, to threaten Cornwallis's flank as he advanced against Washington, made strategic sense, his refusal to respond to Washington's orders bordered on insubordination and his willingness to criticize the commander-in-chief overshadowed whatever other merit his actions might have suggested.

Lambert Cadwalader (1742–1823). Cadwalader was born in Trenton, New Jersey, moving with his family to Philadelphia in 1750. After briefly attending City College he established a successful business with his brother. As a prominent businessman Cadwalader opposed the Stamp Act, was elected to the Provincial Assembly and was appointed to the Philadelphia Committee of Correspondence.

Lambert was appointed captain of militia in 1775 and in early 1776 became lieutenant-colonel of the 3rd Pennsylvania Regiment. He was a veteran of the battles around New York and was captured at Fort

Washington, but released on parole. Cadwalader was instrumental in raising the Philadelphia Associators and commanded the militia unit when it crossed over to New Jersey on December 27, 1776.

It was Cadwalader's decision to cross over to New Jersey after the battle of Trenton that helped galvanize Washington's decision to renew his offensive. Cadwalader and the Associators supplemented the dwindling numbers of Continentals and bolstered Washington's force at Assunpink Creek. Cadwalader's intervention at Princeton saved the remnants of Mercer's Brigade and along with Washington he helped rally the shaken American line.

Edward Hand (1744–1802). Hand was born in Ireland, earning a medical degree at Trinity College, Dublin. He enlisted as a surgeon's mate in the 18th Foot in 1767. The 18th Foot arrived at Philadelphia in July 1767. Hand served at Fort Pitt and resigned his commission in 1774, moving to Lancaster, Pennsylvania. Hand helped organize the Lancaster County Associators and then was commissioned a colonel of the Pennsylvania Line. Hand saw action at the battle of Long Island and the subsequent retreat.

Hand and his men fought a successful delaying action against Cornwallis's advance throughout the day of January 2, 1777. When Brigadier-General Fermoy abandoned his command at Shabakunk Creek, Hand organized the defense that stalled the British and gained valuable time for Washington's defense of Trenton. Hand's riflemen also played a critical role at Princeton, responding to Washington's orders to assist Mercer and Cadwalader.

Major-General Charles Lee shown as a British officer in the French and Indian War. Lee was wounded at Ticonderoga and returned to England. He later served in Portugal, Poland and Russia before returning to America in 1773.

BRITISH

William Howe (1729–1814). Joining the British Army in 1748, William Howe was a veteran of the battles of Louisburg, Quebec and Montreal during the French and Indian War. Promoted to major-general in 1772, Howe was also a Member of Parliament and a Whig. His sympathy for the American cause did not preclude him from commanding the British Army sent to crush the rebellion. Although an innovative commander of light infantry who retrained British forces to fight with greater tactical flexibility, Howe was also responsible for the attack on Bunker Hill, where his tactics were unimaginative and costly. Howe and his brother, Admiral Richard Howe spent most of 1776 trying alternatively to defeat the American Army and negotiate a mediated settlement.

Charles Cornwallis (1738–1805). Cornwallis was educated at Eton and Cambridge and attended a military academy in Turin, Italy. Commissioned in 1756 at the age of 17, he rose to lieutenant-colonel of the 12th Foot by 1761, became colonel of the 33rd Foot in 1766, saw combat in the Seven Years War and was made a major-general in 1775. Although Cornwallis was at heart a Whig, sympathetic to the grievances of the American colonists, he responded to the outbreak of hostilities by arranging an assignment in America. He arrived in April 1776 off the coast of North Carolina and joined Lieutenant-General Henry Clinton in a campaign to capture Charleston, South Carolina, in June 1776 that ended in a defeat so humiliating that it would "scarcely be believed in England." In July 1776 Cornwallis accompanied the British task force back to New York, arriving in time to take command of General William Howe's reserve of Hessian grenadiers, British light infantry and grenadiers. Cornwallis figured prominently in the capture of Lord Sterling's command during the battle of Long Island, although he played no significant role in the battles of Harlem Heights and White Plains.

Sir William Howe, British commander-in-chief. Sir William Howe commanded the British armies during the opening stages of the American Revolution, abandoning Boston in March 1776 after the debacle at Bunker Hill. Howe returned with a large force of British and Hessian troops in June 1776, invading New York and driving the American Army into New Jersey.

Lieutenant-General Charles Cornwallis served under General Howe, leading the pursuit of Washington's Army through New Jersey. Cornwallis underestimated General George Washington at the battle of Assunpink Creek, January 2, 1777, allowing the American Army to steal a march during the night and attack Princeton, New Jersey.

Along with Howe, Cornwallis has been criticized for his deliberate pursuit of Washington's Army retreating across New Jersey. While it could be argued that Howe's actions ranged from aggressive to complacent, Cornwallis operated under inconsistent directives from Howe, which limited his freedom of action. His failure to outflank Washington at Assunpink Creek during the night of January 2, 1777, represented a critical mistake.

Johann Rall (1725–76). Rall was the son of Captain Joachim Rall, who served in the regiment of Major-General von Donop. Rall entered the same regiment in 1740, rising to the rank of major in 1740. Rall transferred out of the regiment and was made colonel of the Mansbach Regiment in January 1772. Rall was a veteran of the Seven Years War, War of Austrian Succession and fought for Catherine the Great against the Turks between 1771 and 1772.

Rall arrived in America as part of the Hesse-Cassel contingent in 1776 and participated in the battles around New York, including Long Island, White Plains and Brooklyn Heights. While Rall made a series of tactical errors leading up to the battle of Trenton, Howe's decision to post Rall in Trenton was fundamentally untenable. Although Rall attempted to alert his superiors to the dangers of his exposed position he ultimately bears the most responsibility for ignoring intelligence that might have allowed him to avoid surprise and the destruction of his command.

OPPOSING ARMIES

In discussing the basic tactical unit fighting in the American Revolution the terms regiment and battalion are, in most cases, interchangeable. Typically one or more battalions made up regiments but in the American Revolution a regiment was usually composed of only a single battalion. American, British and Hessian line infantry units will be referred to as regiments. The only exception will be British light infantry and grenadier units, which were composite units, created by combining the light infantry or grenadier companies of the various British regiments into separate units. The Philadelphia Associators Militia also were organized as battalions. Most Hessian grenadier battalions were also composite units. A grenadier or light infantry battalion was generally the same size as a British line regiment. Hessian *Jäger* usually operated as independent companies, although several companies might be deployed together.

THE AMERICAN ARMY

Continental Regulars

The Continental Army of 1776 was composed of 27 regiments, raised on January 1 from Massachusetts, Connecticut, Rhode Island and New Hampshire. The only exception was Colonel William Thompson's Pennsylvania unit, which was designated the 1st Pennsylvania Continental Infantry Regiment. Their term of enlistment was set to expire on December 31, 1776. Each regiment was organized into eight companies of 76 men, plus officers, noncommissioned officers and musicians. Although some units did include grenadier companies in their initial organizations, the Continental organization did not include grenadier or light infantry companies. Selected regiments, such as the 1st Pennsylvania Continental Regiment, were designated as rifle regiments and acted similarly to the British light infantry battalions or Hessian *Jäger* companies.

The Continental regiments that remained with Washington for the Trenton and Princeton campaign were veterans of the battles around New York. Although many regiments were significantly under strength, they formed the core of Washington's Army. Training of the Continental units suffered from a lack of uniform standards and practices. The quality of the officer corps also varied widely, although the reverses of the late summer and fall had weeded out many of the incompetent officers. Tactically the Continentals formed a two-rank line to maximize their firepower. The Americans were armed with a mix of British, French and domestic muskets. Shortages of muskets were aggravated by the practice of some units of taking

TOP

A collection of American muskets used during the Revolution. American armies were largely dependent on captured British firearms and shipments from both France and Spain, resulting in a wide variety of types used, particularly early in the conflict. (Princeton Battlefield, William Clarke House Museum)

BOTTOM

Powder horns such as these were carried by American militia and sometimes were richly decorated. This one shows the skyline of colonial Boston, suggesting its owner served in a unit besieging the city in 1775 and early 1776. (Princeton Battlefield, William Clarke House Museum)

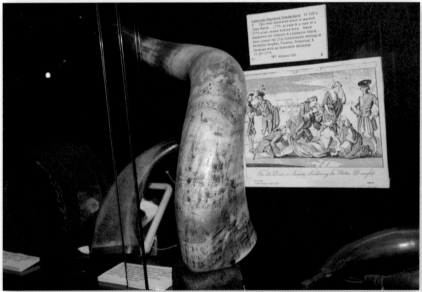

guns with them when their enlistments had expired, although Washington directed that special efforts be made to disarm those men who were mustered out of service. American units also suffered from a shortage of bayonets.

The American rifle units operated as skirmishers, armed with a variety of personal rifles. While these guns were highly accurate in the hands of experienced riflemen they suffered from a slow rate of reloading and lack of a bayonet, making these units vulnerable to British bayonet attacks.

Militia

Although militia units were to play a pivotal role in the campaign their performance was characterized by fits of unmanageable enthusiasm and uncontrollable despair. Throughout the early period of the Revolution Washington engaged in a struggle with the Continental Congress over the composition of the American Army. Washington, perhaps because of this experience with militia during the French and Indian War, believed that only a standing army of trained regulars could have any hope of defeating the British. During the New York campaign the militia had proven themselves unreliable in both their willingness to turn out and in their battlefield performance. Washington wrote Congress on September 25, 1776, stressing that, "to place any dependence upon Militia, is assuredly, resting upon a broken staff." Washington believed that their lack of training and experience "makes them timid and ready to fly from their own Shadows." As American fortunes dimmed in the days after the loss of Fort Washington the New Jersey Militia failed on numerous occasions to respond to the call to assemble.

Militia units were usually organized around a specific geographical site, either counties or towns and villages. The size of the units varied, depending on the population of the area of recruitment. They were usually equipped with personal arms, resulting in a wide range of muskets, rifles and other firearms, most without bayonet.

Some militia units from New Jersey and Pennsylvania did join Washington at points during the campaign and the Philadelphia Associators played a central role in the battle of Assunpink Creek and the first phase of the battle of Princeton. The Associators were first organized in 1747 with the help of Benjamin Franklin, to defend the city from Indian or Spanish attack. In July 1776 the Associators were mustered and operated in New Jersey for six weeks before disbanding. On December 10, 1776, three battalions of foot, complemented by an artillery section and a small troop of horse marched out of Philadelphia to assist Washington. Because they had elementary training together as a unit and sound organization the Associators were more reliable than typical militia units. This reliability was shown during the battle at William Clarke's Farm when they were able to recover quickly from their initial confusion. Major-General Greene, who was highly critical of militia throughout the war, praised the Associators writing that "great credit is due to the Philadelphia Militia ... who behaved exceedingly well considering they were never in action before."

Washington had several mounted militia units available to him, including a mounted company of the Philadelphia Associators, which accompanied him throughout the battles of Trenton and Princeton.

The Trenton and Princeton campaigns also saw the participation of a small company of the newly created United States Marines. This unit was part of Cadwalader's Brigade.

THE BRITISH ARMY

The British Army under General William Howe was composed of infantry regiments, consisting of 10 companies—eight musketeer companies, one grenadier and one light infantry company. Each company was made up of a captain, lieutenant and ensign, with two sergeants, three corporals, a drummer and 38 privates. As a standard practice the grenadier and light infantry companies were separated from their parent regiments and organized as separate battalions. British grenadiers wore tall bearskin helmets rather than the brass grenadier caps worn by the Hessian grenadiers. British light infantry wore short coats and small leather helmets.

Howe also had available to him composite Guard regiments, made up of men from various regiments of Guards in the British Army. Their structure differed from the standard organization, having two battalions, each composed of four center musketeer companies. In addition the 1st Battalion included a grenadier company while the 2nd Battalion included a light infantry company. When deployed in a two-rank line British infantry fought in close, open or extended order. Close order required adjacent men's elbows to touch, while open order allowed an 18in. gap between men and extended order up to a five-foot space between men. General Howe had instituted these flexible tactical formations early in 1776, reflecting his experience in the French and Indian War.

The British employed troops of both the 16th and 17th light dragoons during the campaign. In 1776 these cavalry regiments were organized with six mounted and six dismounted troops. The mounted troops numbered approximately 44 men, while the dismounted troops included 34 men.

British artillery was composed of both 3-pdr and 6-pdr field guns, usually organized as two-gun companies. These artillery companies averaged about 50 men.

Hessians

The Hessians participating in the Trenton and Princeton campaign were part of the Hesse-Cassel contingent that landed on Long Island with Gen. Howe in the summer of 1776. Hesse-Cassel provided 19 regiments along with associated artillery. The typical German infantry regiment at full strength included over 600 men, including noncommissioned officers, musicians and soldiers. Larger in comparison with their British or American counterparts, the Hessian regiment was composed of five companies, four battalion companies and a grenadier company. Hessian regiments were designated as either musketeer or fusilier, the only difference being the fusiliers wore a small miter hat and the musketeers a cocked hat.

Private, Hessian Fusilier Regiment von Lossberg, 1776, as they appeared at Long Island and Trenton, Don Troiani. The British made extensive use of troops hired from Hesse-Cassel. The Fusilier Regiment von Lossberg were part of the Trenton garrison surprised by the American army on December 26, 1776. (Painting by Don Troiani, www.historicalimagebank.com)

Like their British allies the Hessians created composite regiments made up of the grenadier companies from different regiments, reducing each regiment by one company when deployed in the field. Grenadier Regiment Rall was unique in that it was not a composite battalion but rather was a permanent grenadier unit.

The individual regiments were named for their commanding colonel and through the course of the war some regiments changed names as their commanders changed. Others, like the survivors of the Hessian regiments at Trenton, were combined with existing units.

The Hessians also had available light infantry, *Jäger*, recruited from game wardens and hunters and trained to fight in open order. They were used extensively as scouts in the advance across New Jersey. Armed with short European rifles, and wearing dark green coats, each company of *Jäger* included approximately 50 men.

Hessian tactics were similar to those of their British allies. Howe encouraged the Hessians to adopt the two-rank line rather than their traditional three-rank line. Although several of the Hessian units did make the transition, they continued to utilize the close-order formation.

ORDERS OF BATTLE

BATTLE OF TRENTON, DECEMBER 22, 1776

(Note: the totals derived from these December 22, 1776, returns are substantially larger than the estimates of 2,400 men under Washington's command that have been used in previous works. Although desertion and sickness may have accounted for lower troop strength on the evening of December 25, 1776, the size of Washington's force was larger than 2,400.)

American Army

Commander-in-chief Gen. George Washington

Washington's Life Guard—Capt. Caleb Gibbs (75 men)

1st Troop of Philadelphia Light Horse—Capt. Samuel Morris (25 men)

ADVANCE GUARD

Stephen's Brigade—Brig. Gen. Adam Stephen (549 men)

    4th Virginia Continental Regiment—Lt. Col. Robert Lawson (229 men)

    5th Virginia Continental Regiment—Col. Charles Scott (129 men)

    6th Virginia Continental Regiment—Col. Mordecai Buckner (191 men)

GREENE'S DIVISION—MAJ. GEN. NATHANIEL GREENE

Sterling's Brigade—Brig. Gen. Lord Sterling (673 men)

    1st Virginia Continental Regiment—Capt. John Fleming (185 men)

    1st Delaware Continental Regiment—Col. John Haslett (108 men)

    3rd Virginia Continental Regiment—Col. George Weedon (181 men)

    1st Pennsylvania Rifle Regiment—Col. Ennion Williams (199 men)

Mercer's Brigade—Brig. Gen. Hugh Mercer (838 men)

    20th Connecticut Continental Regiment—Col. John Durkee (313 men)

    1st Maryland Continental Regiment—Lt. Col. Francis Ware (163 men)

    27th Massachusetts Continental Regiment—Col. Israel Hutchinson (115 men)

    Connecticut State Troops—Col. Phillip Bradley (142 men)

    Maryland Rifle Battalion—Lt. Col. Moses Rawling (105 men)

Fermoy's Brigade—Brig. Gen. Matthias Alexis Roche de Fermoy (628 men)

    1st Pennsylvania Continental Regiment—Col. Edward Hand (254 men)

    Pennsylvania German Regiment—Col. Nicholas Haussegger (374 men)

SULLIVAN'S DIVISION—MAJ. GEN. JOHN SULLIVAN

Glover's Brigade—Col. John Glover (865 men)

    14th Massachusetts Continental Regiment (Marblehead)—Col. John Glover (177 men)

    3rd Massachusetts Continentals—Col. William Shepard (217 men)

    19th Connecticut Continental Regiment—Col. Charles Webb (212 men)

    23rd Massachusetts Continental Regiment—Col. John Bailey (146 men)

    26th Massachusetts Continental Regiment—Col. Loammi Baldwin (113 men)

Sargent's Brigade—Col. Paul Sargent (827 men)

    16th Massachusetts Continental Regiment—Col. Paul Sargent (152 men)

    22nd Connecticut Continental Regiment—Col. Andrew Ward (157 men)

    6th Battalion Connecticut State Troops—Col. John Chester (260 men) (This regiment did not cross to Trenton on December 26, 1776.)

    13th Massachusetts Continental Regiment—Col. Joseph Reed (122 men)

    1st New York Continental Regiment—Capt. John Johnson (56 men)

    3rd New York Continental Regiment—Lt. Col. Baron Friedrich von Weisenfels (80 men)

St. Clair's Brigade—Brig. Gen. Arthur St. Clair (505 men)
    5th New Hampshire Continental Regiment—Col. John Stark (110 men)
    8th New Hampshire Continental Regiment—Col. Enoch Poor (90 men)
    2nd New Hampshire Continental Regiment—Lt. Col. Israel Gilman (135 men)
    15th Massachusetts Continental Regiment—Col. John Patterson (170 men)

Knox's Regiment of Continental Artillery—Brig. Gen. Henry Knox
    New York Company Continental Artillery—Capt. Sebastian Baumann (80 men with
        three guns)
    Massachusetts Company of Continental Artillery—Capt. Lt. Winthrop Sargent (55 men
        with three guns)
    New York State Company of Artillery—Capt. Alexander Hamilton (36 men with two guns)
    Eastern Company, New Jersey State Artillery—Capt. Daniel Neil (53 men with two guns)
    Western Company, New Jersey State Artillery—Capt. Samuel Hugg (55 men with two guns)
    2nd Company, Pennsylvania State Artillery—Capt. Thomas Forrest (52 men with two
        6-pdr guns)
    2nd Company of Artillery, Philadelphia Associators—Capt. Joseph Moulder (85 men with
        three guns)

Hessian forces

Brigade Rall—Col. Johann Gottlieb Rall (1,356 men)
    Grenadier Regiment Rall—Lt. Col. Balthasar Brethauer, Acting (512 men)
    Fusilier Regiment von Lossberg—Lt. Col. Francis Scheffer, Acting (345 men)
    Fusilier Regiment von Knyphausen—Maj. Friedrich von Dechow (429 men)
    Jäger Company—Lt. Friedrich Wilhelm von Grothausen (50 men)
    16th Light Dragoons (20 men)

BATTLE OF ASSUNPINK CREEK, JANUARY 2, 1777

British forces

CORNWALLIS'S DIVISION—LT. GEN. CHARLES CORNWALLIS (9,500 MEN)

16th Light Dragoons (two troops)
Light Infantry Brigade—Maj. Gen. James Grant
    1st Battalion Light Infantry—Maj. Thomas Musgrave
    2nd Battalion Light Infantry—Maj. John Maitland
    42nd Regiment of Foot (Royal Highland Regiment)—Lt. Col. Thomas Sterling
    71st Regiment of Foot (Scottish Regiment)

British Grenadiers and Guards Brigade—Lt. Col. Henry Monckton
    1st Battalion Grenadiers—Lt. Col. William Medows
    2nd Battalion Grenadiers—Lt Col. Henry Monckton
    2nd Battalion Guards—Lt. Col. James Ogilvie

Royal Artillery—six companies of the 4th Battalion

Hessian Brigade—Col. Carl von Donop
    Grenadier Battalion von Köhler—Lt. Col. Johann Köhler
    Grenadier Battalion von Linsingen—Lt. Col. Otto von Linsing
    Grenadier Battalion von Minnigerode—Lt. Col. Friedrich von Minnigerode
    Grenadier Battalion von Block—Lt. Col. Henrich von Block
    Fusilier Battalion von Loos—Col. Johann von Loos (included survivors of Rall regiment)

Jäger Company—Captain Johann Ewald
Jäger Company—Captain Friedrich Lorey

2nd Brigade—Brig. Gen. Alexander Leslie
  5th Regiment of Foot—Lt. Col. William Walcott
  28th Regiment of Foot—Lt. Col. Robert Prescott
  35th Regiment of Foot—Lt. Col. James Cockburne
  49th Regiment of Foot—Maj. Thomas Dilkes

American forces
Commander-in-chief—Gen. George Washington (10,200 men)

GREENE'S DIVISION—MAJOR-GENERAL NATHANIEL GREENE (1,300 MEN)
Mercer's Brigade—Brig. Gen. Hugh Mercer (300 men)
  1st Maryland Continental Regiment—Capt. John Stone
  1st Pennsylvania Rifle Regiment—Maj. Ennion Williams
  Maryland Rifle Battalion—Lt. Col. Moses Rawling
  1st Delaware Continental Regiment—Col. John Haslett
  1st Virginia Continental Regiment—Capt. John Fleming
  Eastern Company, New Jersey State Artillery—Capt. John Niel

Stephen's Brigade—Col. Charles Scott (400 men)
  4th Virginia Continental Regiment—Lt. Col. Robert Lawson
  5th Virginia Continental Regiment—Maj. Josiah Parker
  6th Virginia Continental Regiment—Maj. Richard Parker

Fermoy's Brigade—Brig. Gen. Matthias Alexis Roche de Fermoy (600 men)
  Pennsylvania German Regiment—Col. Nicholas Haussegger
  1st Pennsylvania Continental Regiment—Col. Edward Hand
  2nd Company, Pennsylvania State Artillery—Capt. Thomas Forrest

SULLIVAN'S DIVISION—MAJ. GEN. JOHN SULLIVAN (1,200–1,400 MEN)
St. Clair's Brigade—Brig. Gen. Arthur St. Clair
Approximately 100 from each of the following units:
  5th New Hampshire Continental Regiment—Col. John Stark
  2nd New Hampshire Continental Regiment—Col. James Reed
  8th New Hampshire Continental Regiment—Col. Enoch Poor
  1st Massachusetts Continental Regiment—Col. John Paterson
  4th Massachusetts Continental Regiment—Col. William Shepard
  19th Connecticut Continental Regiment—Col. Charles Webb
  14th Massachusetts Continental Regiment (Marblehead)—Col. John Glover
  23rd Massachusetts Continental Regiment—Col. John Bailey
  16th Massachusetts Continental Regiment—Col. Paul Sargent
  22nd Connecticut Continental Regiment—Col. Andrew Ward
  6th Battalion Connecticut State Troops—Col. John Chester
  13th Massachusetts Continental Regiment—Col. Joseph Reed
  New York State Company of Artillery—Capt. Alexander Hamilton

INDEPENDENT COMMANDS
Ewing's Brigade of Pennsylvania Militia of the Flying Camp—Brig. Gen. James Ewing (600 men)
  Cumberland County Regiment—Col. Frederick Watts
  Lancaster County Regiment—Col. Jacob Klotz

Cumberland County Regiment—Col. William Montgomery

York County Regiment—Col. Richard McAllister

Chester County Regiment—Col. James Moore

Bucks County Detachment—Col. Joseph Hart

Cadwalader's Philadelphia Associator's Brigade—Brig. Gen. John Cadwalader (1,500 men)

1st Battalion Philadelphia Militia—Col. Jacob Morgan

2nd Battalion Philadelphia Militia—Col. John Bayard

3rd Battalion Philadelphia Militia—Lt. Col. John Nixon

Philadelphia Rifle Battalion—Col. Timothy Matlack

Philadelphia Light Infantry—Capt. George Henry

Kent County Delaware Militia Company—Capt. Thomas Rodney

United States Marine Company—Maj. Samuel Nicholas

2nd Company of Artillery, Philadelphia Associators—Capt. Joseph Moulder

Hitchcock's Brigade—Maj. Israel Angell (350 men)

Lippitt's Rhode Island Regiment—Col. Christopher Lippitt

2nd Rhode Island Continental Regiment—Col. Daniel Hitchcock

1st Rhode Island Continental Regiment—Col. James Varnum

4th Massachusetts Continental Regiment—Col. John Nixon

12th Massachusetts Continental Regiment—Col. Moses Little

Massachusetts Company of Continental Artillery—Capt. Lt. Winthrop Sargent

Mifflin's Brigade—Gen. Thomas Mifflin (1,800 men)

2nd Pennsylvania Continental Regiment—Col. Phillip De Haas

4th Pennsylvania Continental Regiment—Col. Daniel Brodhead

10th Pennsylvania Continental Regiment—Col. Joseph Penrose

11th Pennsylvania Continental Regiement—Col. Richard Humpton

12th Pennsylvania Continental Regiment—Col. William Cooke

Griffin's New Jersey Militia Brigade—Col. Silas Newcombe (500 men)

Cumberland County Militia—Col. Silas Newcombe

Cumberland County Militia—Col. David Potter

Gloucester County Militia—Col. Joseph Ellis

Gloucester County Militia—Col. Richard Somers

Salem County Militia—Col. Samuel Dick

BATTLE OF PRINCETON, JANUARY 3, 1777

British forces

4TH BRIGADE—MAJ. GEN. GRANT (ABSENT) LT. COL. CHARLES MAWHOOD (950 MEN)

17th Regiment of Foot—Lt. Col. Charles Mawhood (246 men)

40th Regiment of Foot—Maj. Samuel Bradstreet (333 men)

55th Regiment of Foot—Maj. Cornelius Cuyler (116 men)

16th Light Dragoons (mounted, one troop, 30 men)

16th Light Dragoons (dismounted, three troops, 90 men)

Grenadiers (one company, 32 men)

Light infantry (one company, 50 men)

42nd Regiment of Foot (Royal Highland Regiment) (one company, 50 men)

Artillery (three sections, six guns)

American forces

Commander-in-chief—General George Washington

GREENE'S DIVISION—MAJOR-GENERAL NATHANIEL GREENE (1,800 MEN)

Mercer's Brigade—Brig. Gen. Hugh Mercer (300 men)

    1st Maryland Continental Regiment—Capt. John Stone

    1st Pennsylvania Rifle Regiment—Maj. Ennion Williams

    Maryland Rifle Battalion—Lt. Col. Moses Rawling

    1st Delaware Continental Regiment—Col. John Haslett

    1st Virginia Continental Regiment—Capt. John Fleming

    Eastern Company, New Jersey State Artillery—Capt. John Niel

Cadwalader's Philadelphia Associator's Brigade—Brig. Gen. John Cadwalader (1,500 men)

    1st Battalion Philadelphia Militia—Col. Jacob Morgan

    2nd Battalion Philadelphia Militia—Col. John Bayard

    3rd Battalion Philadelphia Militia—Lt. Col. John Nixon

    Philadelphia Rifle Battalion—Col. Timothy Matlack

    Philadelphia Light Infantry—Capt. George Henry

    Kent County Delaware Militia Company—Capt. Thomas Rodney

    United States Marine Company—Maj. Samuel Nickolas

    2nd Company of Artillery, Philadelphia Associators—Capt. Joseph Moulder

SULLIVAN'S DIVISION—MAJ. GEN. JOHN SULLIVAN (2,200 MEN)

St. Clair's Brigade—Brig. Gen. Arthur St. Clair (1,200 men)

Elements of the following units:

    5th New Hampshire Continental Regiment—Col. John Stark

    2nd New Hampshire Continental Regiment—Col. James Reed

    8th New Hampshire Continental Regiment—Col. Enoch Poor

    1st Massachusetts Continental Regiment—Col. John Paterson

    4th Massachusetts Continental Regiment—Col. William Shepard

    19th Connecticut Continental Regiment—Col. Charles Webb

    14th Massachusetts Continental Regiment (Marblehead)—Col. John Glover

    23rd Massachusetts Continental Regiment—Col. John Bailey

    16th Massachusetts Continental Regiment—Col. Paul Sargent

    22nd Connecticut Continental Regiment—Col. Andrew Ward

    6th Battalion Connecticut State Troops—Col. John Chester

    13th Massachusetts Continental Regiment—Col. Joseph Reed

    New York State Company of Artillery—Capt. Alexander Hamilton

Fermoy's Brigade—Brig. Gen. Mathias Fermoy (600 men)

    Pennsylvania German Regiment—Col. Nicholas Haussegger

    1st Pennsylvania Continental Regiment—Col. Edward Hand

Hitchcock's Brigade—Maj. Israel Angell (350 men)

    Lippitt's Rhode Island Regiment—Col. Christopher Lippitt

    2nd Rhode Island Continental Regiment—Col. Daniel Hitchcock

    1st Rhode Island Continental Regiment—Col. James Varnum

    4th Massachusetts Continental Regiment—Col. John Nixon

    12th Massachusetts Continental Regiment—Col. Moses Little

    Massachusetts Company of Continental Artillery—Capt. Lt. Winthrop Sargent

OPPOSING PLANS

BRITISH PLANS

Northern New Jersey, 1777, showing Long Island, Staten Island and the highland area. It was across this part of New Jersey that Washington's Army retreated from Fort Lee in late November 1776. Major-General Lee was given command of the largest body of troops and ordered to New Castle, New York, to guard against a British move north.

After the near disastrous retreat from Long Island on August 29, 1776, Washington deployed his army to defend New York. General William Howe arranged his forces opposite Manhattan from Red Hook to Hell Gate but to the surprise of his own officers made no move to cross the East River. During this pause in the British offensive Admiral Richard Howe resumed his peace overtures to the American rebels. Both he and his brother had been assigned as peace commissioners by King George III and throughout the summer and early fall they had attempted through fits and starts both to punish the rebels and offer an olive branch for reconciliation with the Crown. It was a delicate balancing act.

Howe used American Maj. Gen. Sullivan, captured during the battle of Brooklyn, to arrange face-to-face negotiations with representatives of the Continental Congress. On September 11 John Adams, Benjamin Franklin and

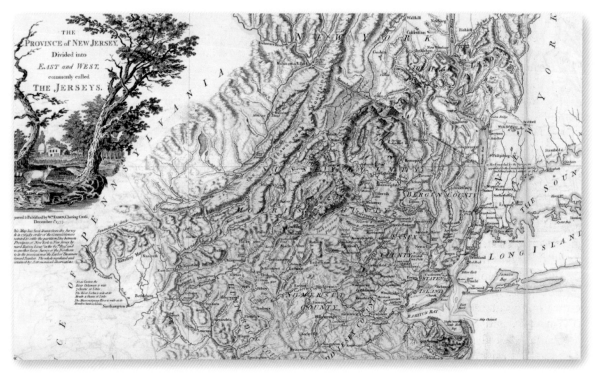

Southern New Jersey, 1777, showing the area along the Delaware River, north of Philadelphia, including Trenton. This map shows the road network available to both Washington and Cornwallis as they maneuvered during early January 1777.

Edward Rutledge met with the Howe brothers on Staten Island. When it became clear that the Howes could not negotiate unless the Americans repudiated the recently adopted Declaration of Independence the talks broke down. With the collapse of this latest round of peace negotiations Gen. Howe shifted back to the offensive and in a series of decisive actions drove Washington from New York City and scattered the American forces.

With the capture of Fort Washington on November 16 and Fort Lee on November 20 the British secured New York City and the Howes contemplated their options. Throughout the campaign around New York Sir Henry Clinton had chafed under what he believed was the dilatory behavior of the Howe brothers. Although Clinton had led the attacks at Long Island and New York his advice to Gen. Howe was regularly ignored. He urged Howe to keep the Americans on the run to no visible effect. The slow and unpredictable pace of Howe's pursuit frustrated Clinton and resulted in increasingly strained relations between the two commanders. Howe's annoyance at Clinton only increased with the fall of Fort Lee and his increasingly strident suggestions that the British should either strike quickly to destroy the tattered remnants of the American Army in New Jersey or move to Philadelphia and capture the Continental Congress.

The Howe brothers would have none of it and rejected Clinton's proposals out of hand in large measure since they were inconsistent with the strategy they had previously agreed upon. The Howes had also discovered by mid-November that General Guy Carleton's offensive of upper New York from Canada had misfired. Howe had considered the juncture with Carleton's

Philadelphia, Pennsylvania, seat of the American Government in 1776. The American capital was ostensibly Howe's ultimate objective as the 1776 campaign came to a close. Washington feared that Howe would try and force a passage over the Delaware River or wait until the river froze over during the winter.

14,000 men the best hope for securing the Hudson River and isolating New England. The American winter was coming on and would subject both the British Army and Royal Navy to increased privations. Captured dispatches also provided important information about the enemy. In them Washington and his staff complained about the indiscipline and declining morale of the army. More importantly the messages detailed Washington's decision to divide his army.

The challenge that faced the Howes was how to secure well-supplied winter quarters, build up their strength over the winter and finish off the rebellious Americans in the spring. The decision reached in early November was to secure the eastern counties of New Jersey, providing access to the resources of the rich farmlands while at the same time finding an appropriate anchorage for the fleet.

The capture of Newport and its warm-water harbor would provide the Navy with the anchorage they needed and also provided a way to rid Howe of the irksome Clinton by putting him in command of the expedition. Securing New Jersey was assigned to Lt. Gen. Charles Cornwallis. He was given strict instructions to pursue the Americans as far as New Brunswick on the Raritan River but no further.

AMERICAN PLANS

Throughout the war Gen. George Washington maintained an increasingly effective system of intelligence gathering. Early in November Washington wrote Maj. Gen. Greene at Fort Lee informing him that he believed the British were intent on invading New Jersey. Further intelligence suggested that the British were collecting a fleet of flat-bottomed boats for the Hudson River crossing and Washington relocated his headquarters to Hackensack, New Jersey, on November 13 to keep in close contact with Greene at Fort Lee. Before leaving White Plains Washington held a conference with his generals and prepared a contingency for the possible British invasion of New Jersey. Washington left Maj. Gen. Charles Lee with approximately 7,000 men at New Castle, New York, to guard against a British move toward New England and

Maj. Gen. Heath with another 3,000 to protect the Hudson highlands. Washington's instructions to Lee were that in the event of a British invasion of New Jersey Lee was to bring his troops south to join Washington and the main army.

As he waited for the next British move Washington faced threats on multiple fronts. Protecting the Hudson River and access to New England were significant considerations. Although Washington knew of Carleton's failed effort to push south he still feared that Howe would move north to secure the Hudson River and threaten New England. Despite his concerns about that possibility his main concern was the protection of Philadelphia. Not knowing exactly where the British thrust into New Jersey would come, Washington dispersed his meager force to guard the extended coastline from Fort Lee south to Perth Amboy.

Washington had detached eight regiments under the command of Major-General William Alexander, also known as Lord Sterling, to guard the New Jersey coast from Amboy to Elizabethtown Point. General Adam Stephen arrived around November 8 with the 4th, 5th and 6th Virginia regiments and was ordered to Perth Amboy. Colonel Hand had 1,200 men stationed between Elizabethtown and Woodbridge to guard the coast. British possession of Staten Island allowed them the possible option of utilizing any one of several good crossings, access to a reliable road network and direct access to Philadelphia. A British attack from Staten Island would outflank the Americans and put the British Army between Washington and Philadelphia, spelling disaster for the Revolution.

Evidence that Washington had long considered the need to retire through New Jersey can be found in the preparations made by Nathaniel Greene. As early as the end of October, Greene had proposed to move supplies from the vulnerable coastal areas to a string of depots along the most likely route of American retreat through New Jersey. Washington approved of the proposal and supplies were moved to Hackensack, Acquackanonk, Elizabethtown, Newark, Springfield, Bound Brook, Princeton and Trenton. While the retreating American forces suffered from exposure to the elements and lack of equipment they were generally well supplied with food.

As his army retreated across the Delaware River, Washington had already begun to consider a possible strike at the British. While the British advance was momentarily stopped by the lack of boats Washington knew the Delaware River was prone to freezing during the winter. If the British were intent on attacking Philadelphia the Delaware was not a permanent obstacle. Most importantly, Washington knew he had to attack soon since the bulk of his veteran units would disappear on January 1, 1777. With no guarantee of success Washington knew this next gamble might be his last.

Raising the new American flag, 1776. Various versions of the American flag, featuring the stars and stripes design were developed during 1775 and 1776. It wasn't until June 1777 that the Continental Congress adopted the final design.

TRENTON AND PRINCETON, VICTORY OR DEATH

RETREAT THROUGH NEW JERSEY

The string of defeats that began with the retreat from Long Island, through the battles around New York, including the loss of forts Washington and Lee, and culminated with the dispirited retreat across the Hackensack River brought Washington to his darkest period as commander-in-chief. Just the day before the loss of Fort Lee Washington wrote his brother, lamenting that "It is impossible for me in the compass of a Letter to give you any Idea of our Situation—of my difficulties—& the constant perplexities and mortifications … I am wearied almost to death with the retrograde Motion of things …"

The continual losses also caused members of the Continental Congress and officers in the army to raise concerns over Washington's judgment and temperament. Major-General Charles Lee, writing to Dr. Benjamin Rush, claimed that "I foresaw, predicted, all that has happened" and that he advised Washington to "draw off the garrison or they will be lost." Lee's comments reflected his growing contempt for Washington's leadership. Even as Washington was shepherding the Fort Lee garrison to safety he made a point of ordering his aide, Lieutenant-Colonel William Grayson to send a message to Lee, notifying him that the British had crossed the Hudson and "His Excellency thinks it would be advisable in you to remove the troops under your command on this side of the North River & there await further orders." Thus began a complicated series of increasingly bitter exchanges between the two leaders. In this complicated minuet Lee sought to delay his juncture with Washington but at the same time give the appearance of compliance with the wishes of his superior. Lee wished to remain at arm's length to guarantee freedom of action and insulate himself from the imminent collapse of Washington's command.

General Washington assigned Major-General Charles Lee the largest contingent of American troops and ordered him to resist any British attempt to advance north from New York. Washington also ordered Lee to march south to join him if the British invaded New Jersey. (Author's collection)

When he broke up the army in early November Washington believed he and Lee had agreed to the plan that clearly required Lee to move south if the British pressed into New Jersey. On November 10, 1776, Washington sent Lee a note, stating "If the enemy should remove the whole or the greatest part of their force, to the West side of Hudson's River, I have no doubt of your following with all possible dispatch."

Washington spent the night of November 21 with his army in Hackensack. After securing Fort Lee, Lt. Gen. Cornwallis ordered British units to move to the Hackensack River at New Bridge. With the capture of Fort Lee Howe sent Cornwallis additional troops including the 2nd and 4th brigades, a battalion of the 71st Foot and elements of the 16th Light Dragoons. With these reinforcements Cornwallis increased his force to over 10,000 men. Washington's 4,000 men found what shelter they could from the rain in houses and barns between the river and Hackensack. Meanwhile, "the British encamped on the opposite side of the river. We could see their fires about one hundred yards apart, gleaming brightly in the gloom of the night, extending some distance below the town and more than a mile towards New Bridge."

Washington briefly considered making a stand along the Hackensack but the river was only 100 to 200ft wide and fordable in many places. On the morning of November 22 Washington left a rearguard to delay the British at New Bridge and ordered a further retreat to the relative safety of the Passaic River. Cornwallis sent a sizable force composed of two light infantry battalions and a Hessian *Jäger* company, reinforced by two British grenadier battalions, commanded by Major-General John Vaughn, to force a passage across the Hackensack River at New Bridge. The Americans occupied the adjacent Hoogland Tavern and, while the British light infantry and *Jäger* engaged in a short but bitter fight at New Bridge, the bulk of the American Army marched to Acquackanonk Landing and crossed the Passaic River on a dilapidated wooden bridge. The Americans destroyed the bridge as the horsemen of the 16th Light Dragoons followed cautiously. Washington's men suffered through another night in the cold rain. Washington usually rode at the end of the struggling column cajoling his men to keep up. Lieutenant James Monroe, future President of the United States, "saw him … at the head of a small band, or rather in its rear, for was always near the enemy and his countenance and manner made an impression on me which I can never efface."

Cornwallis remained in Hackensack with the main army for two days. British foraging parties fanned out to collect supplies from the surrounding countryside, marveling at the abundance. Despite strict orders against pillaging British and Hessian troops were indiscriminate in their rough treatment of the civilians. The abuses against both rebel and loyalist did nothing to endear the British to the citizens of New Jersey and worked against the Howe brothers' attempts to bring the Americans back to the Crown. British scouts reported large quantities of abandoned equipment littering the route of retreat.

Before leaving Acquackanonk Landing Washington wrote New Jersey Governor William Livingston, requesting yet again the New Jersey Militia assemble to resist the British invasion. Retiring from Acquackanonk Landing the American Army reached Newark on November 23. Major-General Sterling's command, composed of the 1st Delaware, 3rd Virginia and 1st Virginia regiments, advanced to Elizabethtown from New Brunswick to support Washington's main force.

The Continental Congress, informed of the loss of Fort Lee on November 22 formed a committee that met with Washington in New Jersey where Congressional President John Hancock authorized Washington to draw down troops from the Northern Department on November 24. In turn Washington dispatched Brigadier-General Thomas Mifflin to Philadelphia to report to Congress on the condition of the army and dispatched Joseph Reed to Governor Livingston and the New Jersey legislature to renew his appeal for more manpower. Mifflin's report from Philadelphia was not encouraging, describing the Pennsylvanians as "divided and lethargic." Ominously, Washington received no news from Reed.

Brigadier-General Thomas Mifflin was sent by Washington to Philadelphia in late November 1776 to report to Congress on the state of the army. Mifflin reported back to Washington that both Congress and the city were terrified of the British advance.

Colonel Joseph Reed was a close confidant of Washington during 1776. Discouraged by American reverses Reed engaged in questionable correspondence with Maj. Gen. Lee, resulting in his estrangement from Washington. Reed provided Washington with critical information on the road network between Trenton and Princeton.

Thomas Paine served in the Continental Army during the retreat across New Jersey. Paine was the author of the widely read pamphlet *Common Sense*. In response to the faltering fortunes of the American Army Paine penned *The American Crisis*, published in December 1776.

On November 26 Washington requested that General Phillip Schuyler dispatch reinforcements from his Northern Department to join the main army in New Jersey. Seven regiments, totaling approximately 1,200 men were ordered south on December 2. These reinforcements included Vose's Brigade, composed of Greaton's 24th Massachusetts Regiment, Bond's 25th Massachusetts Regiment and Porter's Massachusetts Regiment. A brigade under the command of Brigadier-General Horatio Gates, including Reed's 2nd New Hampshire Regiment, Stark's 5th New Hampshire Regiment, Poor's 8th New Hampshire Regiment and Patterson's 15th Massachusetts Regiment were also included.

At Newark, a farming center of approximately 140 dwellings and 3,000 inhabitants on the west bank of the Passaic River, Washington faced a decision. He could follow the road northwest to Morristown and protect the army from further attack but expose the bulk of New Jersey to British occupation. This would in all likelihood cause Philadelphia to be lost. Washington held a council of war to review his options and spoke to officers individually about the state of the Army. After the reverses of the late summer and fall Washington was not surprised to find pessimism and despair, but he also found springs of optimism. Samuel Webb, aide de camp and secretary to Washington wrote to Joseph Trumbull that "I can only say that no lads ever shew greater activity in retreating than we have since we left you. Our soldiers are the best fellows in the World at this Business …" it was "a sacred truth they never yet have ventured to Attack Us but with great Advantages; they pursue no faster than their heavy artillery can be brought up. With this they scour every piece of Wood, Stone Walls, &c, before they approach. If they come soon we shall give a good acct to our Country."

Another who watched the American Army assemble at Newark was Thomas Paine, who served as a volunteer aide on Maj. Gen. Greene's staff. Paine, the author of the widely read pamphlet *Common Sense*, had suffered through the hasty retreat from Fort Lee. Inspired by the spirit he saw in his fellow soldiers Paine wrote spent most nights writing on a drumhead by firelight. *The American Crisis*, published on December 19, in the *Philadelphia Journal*, opened with the dramatic observation that, "These are the times that try men's souls. The summer soldier and the sunshine patriot will, in this crisis, shrink from the service of their county; but he that stands it now, deserves the love and the thanks of man and woman."

Although Washington's Army was exhausted, many without proper clothes, weapons or equipment it had grown to nearly 5,400 as he gathered in outlying detachments. While his scouts kept watch on the British at Hackensack Washington hoped that the time spent in Newark would allow more New Jersey Militia to come to his aide. In this he was to be bitterly disappointed. More vexing than the militia's failure though was the continuing reluctance of Maj. Gen. Lee to join Washington.

When Washington sent off his letter of November 21 to Lee he was deferential in his language, noting that "It must be painful to you as well as to us to have no news to send you but of a melancholy nature." After explaining the quickly developing situation the best Washington could muster was to suggest "upon the whole therefore, I am of Opinion and the Gentlemen about me concur in it, that the publick Interest requires your coming over to this side, with the Continental troops." Washington closed the letter by suggesting that "unless therefore some new Event should occur, or some more cogent Reason present itself I would have you move over by the easiest and best Passage." This was hardly language to be interpreted as definitive orders by a man desperate to remain apart from his commander-in-chief.

Unknown to Washington at the time was that another letter, from his long time confidant, Joseph Reed, was included in the dispatch case with the courier. Reed, who held the rank of lieutenant-colonel and was adjutant general, had no little contempt for the general officers around Washington, including Nathaniel Greene and Henry Knox. Reed blamed the ill-advised decision to defend New York and the subsequent loss of Fort Washington on these amateur soldiers. In contrast Reed marveled at Lee's obvious experience, the confidence he engendered in fellow officers and the common soldier.

In his letter posted on November 21 Reed despaired about the loss of Fort Washington and how Gen. Washington vacillated until "the blow was struck." "Oh! General, an indecisive mind is one of the greatest misfortunes that can befall an army; how often I lamented it this campaign. All circumstances considered, we are in a very awful and alarming situation, one that requires the utmost wisdom and firmness of mind" Reed wrote.

Lee had already taken steps to try and create a separate identity from Washington, writing to Massachusetts' politicians to propose the idea of two independent armies. He maintained that if his force remained east of the Hudson River it would provide safety to New England. At the same time Lee proposed to Maj. Gen. William Heath that since Washington's message included only a suggestion rather than a direct order that Heath should detach 2,000 men and await further instructions. Heath understood that he was not under Lee's direct command and his previous instructions from Washington could only be altered by a direct order from the commander-in-chief and told Lee so. Lee was not dissuaded and on November 23 announced "I intend to take 2,000 of your division with me into the Jersies; so I must desire that you will have that number in readiness by the day after tomorrow when I shall be with you early in the forenoon."

Heath was unperturbed and on November 24 replied simply that "I conceive it to be my duty to obey my orders." He also described the exchange with Lee in a letter to Washington, who replied on November 25 that he did not intend that any of Heath's men should be detached as proposed by Lee. While Heath's letter added fuel to the now-smoldering fire Washington had already determined that Lee's behavior was bordering on the intolerable.

On November 24 Washington reviewed a letter written by Lee to Josesph Reed, in which he laid out various spurious reasons he could not cross the Hudson River and that he had directed Maj. Gen. Heath to detach 2,000 men. In response Washington wrote:

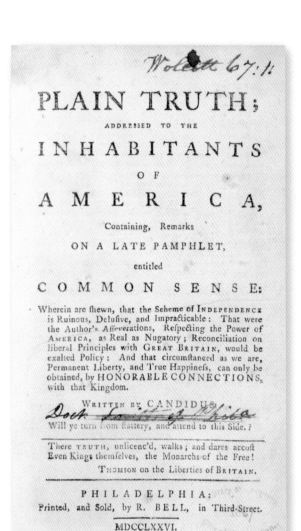

Common Sense, written by Thomas Paine and published anonymously in January 1776, outlined the causes of the American revolt and advocated immediate independence.

The retreat across New Jersey, November 20 to December 7, 1776

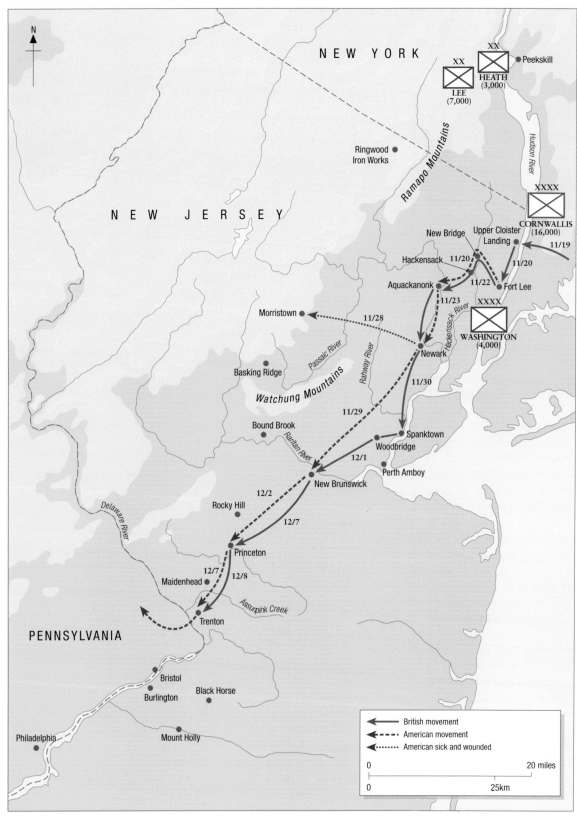

I perceive by your letter to Colo. Reed, that you have entirely mistaken my views in ordering Troops from Genl. Heath's Division to this Quarter. The posts and passes in the Highlands, are of such infinite importance, that they should not be subjected to the least possible degree of risk ... it was your division which I wanted & I wish to march.

Washington, in a growing state of pique, reiterated his order to Lee in response to his increased equivocation on November 27: "My former letters are so full and explicit as to the necessity of your marching as early as possible, that it is unnecessary to add more on that Head. I confess I expected you would have been sooner in motion."

Lee finally agreed to cross the Hudson on December 2 but added that "I shou'd be glad to receive your instructions but I cou'd wish you wou'd bind me as little as possible—not from any opinion, I do assure you, of my own parts—but from a perswasion that detach'd Generals cannot have too great a latitude—unless they are very incompetent indeed." Lee also complained that his men lacked the shoes and blankets necessary for a prolonged march.

As he passed through Peekskill, New York, Lee made one final run at securing a portion of Heath's command. After challenging Heath's refusal to detach 2,000 men Lee ordered Heath's adjutant Major Ebenezer Huntington to prepare orders transferring two regiments to his command. Heath's response was "issue such orders at your own peril." Although Lee was ultimately successful in having the units reassigned he apparently had second thoughts. On December 1 as he moved his men toward the Hudson Lee stopped at Heath's headquarters and announced "upon further consideration, I have concluded not to take the two regiments with me ..." In no small understatement Heath wrote "this conduct of General Lee's appeared not a little extraordinary and one is almost at a loss to account for it."

As this drama was being played out the British and Hessians reorganized at Hackensack and Gen. Howe met with Lt. Gen. Cornwallis to discuss their next moves. Howe's original intent was to stop at Hackensack but the apparent disintegration of Washington's Army, coupled with the bounty of the New Jersey countryside suggested further advances might be useful. Accordingly Cornwallis marched out of Hackensack on November 26 and occupied Acquackanonk, only nine miles from Newark and the American Army. The next day British cavalry and light infantry advanced to the village of Second River while Cornwallis received additional reinforcements in the form of three Hessian regiments commanded by Colonel Johann Gottlieb Rall.

The general attitude of the British command was summed up in a letter written by Lord Rawdon:

You see, my dear sir, that I have not been mistaken in my judgment of this people. The southern people will no more fight than the Yankees. The fact is that their army is broken all to pieces and the spirits of their leaders and their abettors is also broken ... one may venture to pronounce that it is well nigh over with them.

On November 28 after spending five days resting at Newark, Washington directed the sick and wounded be moved to Morristown and the main army was ordered to march roughly 25 miles to New Brunswick, reaching the village at noon on November 29. In addition to news that Cornwallis was on the move Washington had begun to receive troubling intelligence that the

In March 1776 Alexander Hamilton joined the New York Artillery and was commissioned a captain. Hamilton's New York Company fought around New York and retreated with Washington across New Jersey.

British were collecting wagons on Staten Island for a move to Perth Amboy, New Jersey. This was the move that Washington feared, which would expose his army to grave danger.

The British advanced against New Brunswick in two columns. Colonel von Donop commanded the right column, composed of Hessian grenadiers, British infantry, two companies of *Jäger* and a company of 6-pdr artillery. Cornwallis led the left column, composed of British units and the baggage. The British advance guard entered Newark as the American rear guard retired from the town. The Americans retreated from Newark in two columns. One retired through Elizabethtown and Woodbridge while the other marched through Springfield and Quibbletown.

Washington and Cornwallis both pushed their forces on relentlessly. Washington's rearguard kept the British from advancing too quickly, felling trees and engaging in brief firefights with their pursuers. The Americans were experienced at giving the appearance of making a determined stand, causing the British to suspend their advance and deploy their forces, including artillery. Having gained valuable time for the retreating column the Americans disappeared, retiring to another defensive position and repeating the strategy.

New Brunswick was strategically situated along the best road between Philadelphia and New York and included a supply depot at which Washington hoped the New Jersey Militia would be mustering. The American forces reached New Brunswick at noon on November 29.

When he arrived at New Brunswick Washington still despaired of the whereabouts of Lee's Division. Dispatches from Lee to Joseph Reed, who was absent on his mission to the New Jersey legislature, were waiting. Thinking it official correspondence that would shed light on Lee's situation Washington opened the letter. What he found was a personal note from Lee to Reed that began, "I have received your most obliging, flattering letter—lament with you that fatal indecision of mind which in war is a much greater disqualification than stupidity or even want of personal courage. Accident may put a decisive blunder in the right, but eternal defeat and miscarriage must attend the men of the best parts if cursed with indecision."

The letter continued with Lee's now predictable litany of reasons he could not march to Washington's aid. Washington shook off the shock of Reed's betrayal and sent the letter on to Reed with a note explaining that he had opened it by mistake and that he hoped his mission had been successful.

An unintended benefit of Lee's insubordination was that Cornwallis could not completely discern his intentions. As the British left Newark on November 29 Cornwallis ordered Ewald's company of *Jäger* to scout in the direction of Springfield. The next day Cornwallis reinforced Ewald with troopers from the 16th Light Dragoons. Later in the day the 2nd Battalion Light Infantry commanded by Major Maitland joined them at Connecticut Farms Meeting and together they screened the right flank of Cornwallis's advancing column. Finding no sign of Lee's troops, Ewald and Maitland rejoined the main force as it approached New Brunswick on December 1.

While at New Brunswick the American Army shrank as enlistments for some units of the Flying Camp ended on December 1. Just over 2,000 men were free to leave on that day and almost another 1,000 were expected to leave on December 31. Brigadier-General Beall's Maryland Brigade and Brigadier-General Heard's Brigade of New Jersey Flying Camp left on December 1. No amount of pleading from Washington could convince the

bulk of the militia to extend their service. The militia who remained began to slink away and Washington ordered patrols to watch the crossings of the Delaware River for deserters. On that Sunday morning he wrote "Two brigades left us at Brunswick not withstanding the enemy are within two hours march and coming on."

Washington sullenly penned another in a series of increasingly desperate notes to Maj. Gen. Lee, noting "The force I have with me is infinitely inferior in numbers and such as cannot give or promise the least successful opposition. I must entreat you to hasten your march as much as possible or your arrival may be too late to answer any valuable purpose." While writing to John Hancock around 1.30 pm, December 1, Washington declared, "The enemy are fast advancing. Some of them are in sight."

After sending off his supplies and baggage Washington deployed his dwindling force along the Raritan River. There was no bridge over the Raritan at New Brunswick but a partially demolished span crossed the river at Raritan Landing, two miles away. As the British wheeled their artillery into position and engaged in a long-range duel with Captain Alexander Hamilton's Independent Company of New York State Artillery, local Tories led the Hessian *Jäger* toward Raritan Landing. American riflemen kept the *Jäger* at bay throughout the late afternoon.

At the same time Washington dispatched Colonel Richard Humpton's 11th Pennsylvania Regiment to Trenton to secure all the boats that could be found. He was directed to pay particular attention to the Durham boats, flat-bottomed vessels designed to carry large loads across the river. At sundown the American rearguard was ordered to retire 13 miles to Kingston. Washington remained with the Delaware Regiment, which formed the rearguard, long into the night before riding to Princeton. After the Americans withdrew the *Jäger* cautiously established a small bridgehead across the Raritan and Cornwallis's troops settled down opposite New Brunswick while the bridge was repaired.

Small islands like these were found along the Delaware River. Washington used these islands, found near McKonkey's Ferry, to hide the boats that were used to carry the American Army across the river on the evening of December 25, 1776. (Author's collection)

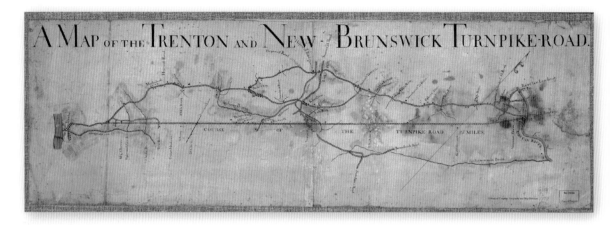

A Map of the Trenton and New - Brunswick Turnpike-Road.

This map of the Trenton and New Brunswick turnpike shows the road network over which Washington retreated in early December 1776. In late December 1776 and early January 1777 Washington marched to Trenton and then to Princeton.

Cornwallis wrote "I could not have pursued the enemy from Brunswick with any prospect of material advantage or without greatly distressing the troops under my command." Cornwallis was also plagued with lingering doubts about the location of Maj. Gen. Lee and his detachment, estimated at 10,000 men. Concerned that Lee was lurking somewhere on his flank Cornwallis deployed his men in strong defensive positions around New Brunswick on December 2 and remained there, under orders, until December 6 when Gen. Howe joined them, bringing Maj. Gen. Grant's Brigade from Perth Amboy with him. Howe also brought with him a change of plans. In early December Howe's men had captured a message from Washington to the Board of War, in which he detailed the expiration of enlistments for the American forces and lamented that he expected few to extend their enlistments.

On December 2 Washington directed the main body of the Army to retreat to Trenton and prepare to retire across the Delaware River. Worried about a continued British pursuit Washington left two brigades, consisting of the Virginia regiments and Haslett's Delawares, totaling about 1,200 men, in Princeton under the command of Lord Sterling. His concern was unnecessary since Howe and Cornwallis lingered at New Brunswick until December 7.

During this period Washington moved his troops and supplies across the Delaware River. While at Trenton additional troops joined Washington's Army. Colonel Nicholas Haussegger's Pennsylvania and Maryland German Regiment, totaling 410 men, were the first to respond to Washington's call for reinforcements. Brigadier-General Mifflin succeeded in raising several battalions of militia, the Associators of the City and Liberties of Philadelphia, totaling 1,500 men. Led by the 1st Troop of Philadelphia Light Horse they joined Washington as the evacuation was in progress. Many of the militia sailed up the Delaware River in a flotilla of boats. The American artist Charles Wilson Peale, who commanded a company of the militia, described the scene as "the most hellish scene I ever beheld. All the shores were lighted up with large fires, boats continuously passing and repassing, full of men, horses, artillery and camp equipage ... The Hollooing of hundreds of men in their difficulties of getting Horses and artillery out of the boats, made it rather the appearance of Hell than any earthly scene."

The Americans maintained effective control over the Delaware River with the help of the Pennsylvania Navy, commanded by Commodore Thomas Seymour. The Navy consisted of 13 galleys or gondolas. Each was equipped with a cannon in the bow and these boats provided important protection to Washington's forces as they crossed to the western shore.

The Pennsylvania Council of Safety ordered Captain Thomas Houston, with the river galley *Warren*, to collect all boats from the New Jersey side of the Delaware. The New Jersey Militia did the same north of Trenton and for a distance of 40 miles the British were denied all manner of boats.

On December 3 Washington described the state of the army in a letter to John Hancock. He also noted that "I have not heard a word from Maj. Gen. Lee since the 26th, which surprises me not a little, as I have dispatched daily expresses to him desiring to know when I might look for him." Washington then ordered Col. Humpton north to find both Lee and the detachments from the Northern Department.

Shaking off their lethargy Howe and Cornwallis resumed their advance on December 7. Leaving two battalions of Guards in New Brunswick to protect the supplies, the British marched in three columns toward the American rearguard at Princeton. That same day Washington, having successfully sent his supplies across the river and somewhat puzzled by the British inactivity at New Brunswick, marched toward Princeton with 1,200 men. Maj. Gen. Greene had been sent to Princeton on December 6 to take command of the forces there. Washington's move toward Princeton was brief. Major-General Greene sent a dispatch rider to warn him of the British advance and he immediately retired to Trenton and sent his men over the river. Greene, with Sterling's brigade in tow, retired to Trenton late in the day and completed the crossing of the Delaware by the morning of December 8.

The British spent the night of December 7 in Princeton and the next day continued their advance to Trenton, finding the Americans had already crossed the Delaware River and abandoned New Jersey. The Hessian *Jäger* and light infantry reached the shore as the last American boats were making their way to safety. Howe and his aides joined the troops near the shore and were placed under "terrific" fire from American batteries across the river, which killed and wounded several but left the British high command untouched.

Cornwallis and his column had halted at Maidenhead, six miles from Trenton. Local Tories had told Cornwallis that boats could be found at Coryell's Ferry, 16 miles north of Trenton. Cornwallis ordered his force, consisting of the 42nd Foot, three battalions of light infantry, two battalions of grenadiers and two foot regiments to march at 1.00am on December 9 to capture them. The British were sorely disappointed to find no boats of any kind and marched later that day to Pennington, five miles northeast of Trenton. Several other attempts to procure boats also ended in frustration.

With his withdrawal into Pennsylvania Washington had preserved the remnants of his army but desperately needed reinforcements. On December 8 Lee, whose force was now between 3,000 and 4,000 men as a result of the expiration of enlistments, crossed the Hudson and marched to Morristown. He now believed that by remaining apart from Washington he could operate on the British flank and even suggested a direct attack against their lines of communication. Cornwallis had thought enough of a possible attack on his rear that he left a brigade in Amboy. On December 10 Howe's Hessian aide-de-camp, Captain Levin Friedrich Ernst von Munchhausen, wrote "General Lee, who is in our rear, makes our support line very unsafe. He often sends out raiding parties. Last night one of them captured a small escort with eight baggage wagons." The next day he related "The support lines behind us become more and more unsafe because of General Lee, who is very audacious. He has captured several patrols and individual dragoons with letters and has taken 700 oxen and nearly 1,000 sheep and hogs from our commissariat."

Major-General Nathaniel Greene showed his aptitude for logistics by convincing Washington to pre-position supplies along the anticipated line of retreat through New Jersey. Greene also commanded the northern force that attacked Trenton on December 26, 1776.

Washington, who had already begun to consider options for a counterstroke, was unconvinced and stressed his need for Lee to join him. Washington responded to Lee on December 10 disapproving of "your hanging on the Rear of the Enemy." Washington had sent Major Robert Hoops off on December 7 in search of Lee with directions for his crossing the Delaware River. Washington directed Lee to cross the Delaware well above Trenton to avoid any contact with the British. Lee responded again by making a case for staying on the British flank and proposed that if the British crossed the Delaware he could drive south to Burlington, New Jersey, and then cross the river. Washington could hardly contain his amazement and wrote on December 14:

> I am much surprised that you should be in any doubt respecting the Route you should take after the information you have had upon that Head as well by Letter from Majr Hoops who was dispatched for the purpose. A large number of boats was procured and is still retained at Tinnicum under a strong guard to facilitate your passage across the Delaware.

Even before receiving this message, on December 12 Lee apparently bowed to the inevitable and ordered his force to join Washington. Lee ordered Maj. Gen. John Sullivan to march the next morning for the rendezvous with Washington. That night Lee left his troops, taking his aide-de-camp, Major William Bradford, Major James Wilkinson, an aide to Major-General Horatio Gates, two French officers and a guard of 15 men three miles to Basking Ridge to spend the night at a tavern. Early on the morning of December 13 a patrol of the 16th Light Dragoons, led by Lieutenant-Colonel William Harcourt, were told by a Tory that Maj. Gen. Lee was close by. After capturing two sentries a mile from the Tavern, Harcourt dispatched Cornet Banastre Tarleton with several men to gather more information. Tarleton captured a courier who confirmed that he had just left Lee. Harcourt moved his patrol toward the Tavern where Lee slept. At 10.00am, as Lee was finishing another letter criticizing Washington's leadership, this one addressed to Maj. Gen. Gates, Harcourt's men attacked. Lee's guards were killed or wounded and the entire force was trapped in the tavern. Harcourt threatened to burn down the tavern unless Lee surrendered. He agreed, and was whisked to New Brunswick, a prisoner of the British, while Bradford, Wilkinson and one French officer escaped.

Washington's reaction to Lee's capture was understated. "I will not comment on the melancholy intelligence ... only adding that I sincerely regret Genl Lee's unhappy fate and feel much for the loss of my County in his Captivity." The British reaction was anything but muted. Lieutenant-Colonel Harcourt claimed Lee was "the most active and enterprising of the enemy's generals." Tarleton was even more effusive, writing to his mother that "this is a most miraculous event—it appears like a dream." Lee's capture reinforced the prevailing opinion among the British leadership that the end of the American Army was inevitable and no further military actions were warranted.

The capture of Lee only added another calamity to the growing list of reverses suffered by the Americans. On December 11 the Continental Congress, alarmed by the

Major-General John Sullivan served under Maj. Gen. Lee during his leisurely march south to join Washington. In mid-December Sullivan was ordered by Lee to march to join Washington. The next day the British captured Lee at Basking Ridge. (Author's collection)

British advance, abandoned Philadelphia and relocated to Baltimore, Maryland. Washington voiced his strong objection. Writing his cousin Lund on December 17 Washington was very clear that "Our only dependence now is upon the speedy enlistment of a new army. If this fails, I think the game will be pretty well up, as, from disaffection and want of spirits and fortitude, the inhabitants, instead of resistance, are offering submission and taking protection from Gen. Howe in New Jersey."

Washington was referring to the recent proclamation by the British for reconciliation. On November 30 Admiral Richard Howe deemed the time right to appeal again to the king's subjects for an end to the rebellion. He issued a proclamation offering full pardon to all those who had taken up arms against the king provided they took an oath of allegiance to his majesty within 60 days from that date. In the first week after the proclamation 3,000 New Jersey adult males availed themselves of the opportunity. The British were also emboldened enough by the response to begin recruiting a fourth battalion for the New Jersey Volunteers.

General Howe, having driven the Americans across the Delaware declared the campaign at an end. He had every reason to believe the campaign was over. He knew the American Army was in tatters, with the next round of enlistments to end by January 1, the most dangerous enemy leader was his captive and his army now had access to the vast resources of New Jersey. Crossing the Delaware would require the construction of new boats. His men, although still enthusiastic and willing to pursue the Americans, had suffered from a lack of supplies and needed to refit. Despite the relatively good weather so far the American winter was approaching and the rules of warfare dictated the army should go into winter quarters. On December 13 he announced his decision to his staff and the next day traveled to New York with Cornwallis, who was to sail for England.

Meanwhile Washington distributed his forces along the Delaware reflecting his continuing concern that the British were planning a thrust toward Philadelphia. The Pennsylvania Flying Camp, led by Brig. Gen. James Ewing and the Philadelphia Associators, 1,200 strong, commanded by Brigadier-General John Cadwalader, had bolstered Washington's numbers. Washington's challenge was how to defend adequately the 70-mile riverfront. The troops were given a three-day ration and directions to a rendezvous point in case the British succeeded in crossing the river. As several of his officers complained, in trying to defend everything Washington could defend nothing.

He placed his main force, the brigades of Sterling, Mercer, de Fermoy and Stephen, along the Delaware River from Yardley's Ferry to Coryell's Ferry. Small earthworks were erected to protect the various ferry crossings. South of Yardley's Ferry to the ferry opposite Bordentown Washington deployed the remnants of Ewing's Pennsylvania Flying Camp and Brigadier-General Dickinson's New Jersey Militia. Brigadier-General John Cadwalader's Pennsylvania Militia extended the American line further south to Dunk's Ferry. Cadwalader's command included 130 United States Marines, part of the four companies recently organized in Philadelphia.

Colonel von Donop assembled a force consisting of approximately 400 Hessian grenadiers and 100 *Jäger* on December 10 and marched 17 miles to Burlington on the Delaware River. The Pennsylvania Navy patrolled this portion of the river and Commodore Seymour vowed to bombard the village

On December 13, 1776, General Lee and several aides were surrounded at a tavern at Basking Ridge, New Jersey. A force of British light dragoons that included Banastre Tarleton captured Lee.

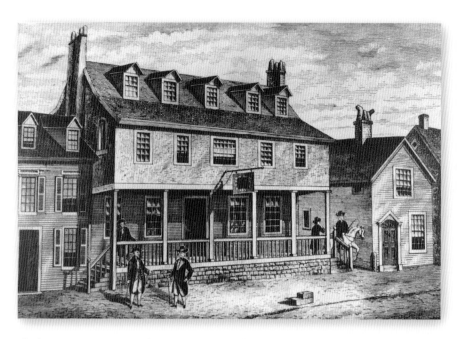

if the enemy occupied it. Donop and his men spent several hours in Burlington before withdrawing. True to his word Seymour bombarded Burlington for several hours after the Hessian departure. Donop later wrote to Brigadier-General Alexander Leslie in Princeton, "I am waiting with impatience the arrival of the Grenadier Battalion Koehler which will bring with them six eighteen-pounders, after which I will take possession of Burlington, where there are according to reports eight to ten gondolas. We will see what resistance they will make to our heavy artillery."

Similarly, Howe deployed his forces to defend New Jersey. He designated Col. von Donop as overall commander of the forward posts, which included Trenton and Bordentown. Colonel Rall lobbied actively to be allowed to occupy Trenton with his regiment, Colonel Francis Scheffer's Fusilier Regiment von Lossberg, and the Fusilier Regiment von Knyphausen, commanded by Major von Dechow. Donop believed the exposed nature of Trenton mitigated against occupation in force but required an outpost of no more than 150 men. Although inclined to agree with Donop, Howe was also sensitive to the need to reward Rall for his leadership at White Plains and Fort Washington. With Howe's agreement Rall deployed his regiment and the Fusilier Regiment von Knyphausen in Trenton on December 12; the Fusilier Regiment von Lossberg arrived on December 14. These men were also joined by a company of artillery, six 3-pdr guns and a detachment of light dragoons. At Trenton, Rall established his headquarters in the Potts House on King Street and settled into a pattern of staying up into the early morning and not waking until mid-morning.

Disappointed that he had been overruled Donop directed Rall to construct redoubts to improve his defenses and then rode south to join the 1,500 men under his direct control at his headquarters in Bordentown. Bordentown was able to accommodate only a single battalion of grenadiers requiring the remainder of Donop's command, two battalions of grenadiers, a detachment of *Jäger* from Captain Ewald's 2nd Company and six 3-pdr cannon to be dispersed along the approaches to the village. One group of *Jäger* was posted two miles north of Bordentown along the road to Trenton and a second group in a mill south of Bordentown along the Delaware. The 42nd Foot Regiment, commanded by Brigadier-General Robert Sterling, and the Hessian Grenadier battalion von Block were stationed in Burlington.

The remainder of the British posts were in Princeton, Hillsborough, New Brunswick, and then reached back toward New York. The deployments, scattered as they were, seemed safe enough to Howe and Cornwallis given their belief that Washington's Army was in tatters. Howe did admit that "the chain I own is rather too extensive ..." With Cornwallis on his way to England Howe left the overall command of his forces, now strung out along a 80-mile line in New Jersey, in the care of Maj. Gen. James Grant, headquartered in New Brunswick.

Washington settled down initially at Colvin's Ferry, later moving 10 miles to William Keith's house to be closer to Greene and Sterling's headquarters. He instructed his commanders to pursue vigorously the collection of intelligence from New Jersey, suggesting that:

> Particular inquiry should be made by the person sent, if any preparations are making to cross the river; whether any boats are building and where; whether they are coming over land from Brunswick; whether any great collections of horses is made, and for what purpose. Expense must not be spared in procuring such intelligence and it will readily be paid by me.

On December 7 Washington ordered Heath, fresh from his encounter with Maj. Gen. Lee, to move his detachment into northern New Jersey. Heath determined that the Loyalist 4th Battalion of New Jersey Volunteers controlled most of the area around Hackensack. He attacked the small British garrison at Hackensack on December 14 and seized considerable stores, which he carried back to his camp at Paramus. New York Militia commanded by Brigadier-General George Clinton joined Heath on December 19 and together they attacked a Loyalist camp at Bergen Woods, capturing 16 men from the New Jersey Volunteers. In response to these attacks Howe was forced to reinforce his eastern New Jersey outposts. However, political pressure from New York forced Heath to return to Peekskill on December 23.

In northern New Jersey a large militia force gathered in Morristown. Lee's detachment had marched though Morristown on December 11 but did not pause. Several days later, on December 14, Brigadier-General Alexander McDougall, who had delayed marching with Lee's main force because of illness arrived in Morristown. On December 17 a detachment of New England Continentals under Lieutenant-Colonel Joseph Vose arrived. At the same time to the east the militia were engaged in a fight with Brig. Gen. Leslie. Leslie, commanding a force of 800 men, was dispatched by Howe in response to rumors of a buildup of militia around Morristown. Three miles east of Chatham, at Bryant's Tavern, the Eastern Battalion of Morris County Militia, commanded by Colonel Jacob Ford, Jr. skirmished with Leslie's troops late on December 17. Expecting to renew the fighting the next day the militia commanders requested that McDougall order Vose to add his Continentals to the growing militia force. On his own initiative McDougall agreed and Vose's men marched to Chatham early on December 18 only to find Leslie had retired. With McDougall's health uncertain Washington sent Brigadier-General William Maxwell to take command of the militia and Vose, and harass the enemy. In the process Maxwell was to establish a firm base at Morristown that would figure prominently as events were to unfold.

British winter quarters and American defensive dispositions, December 23, 1776

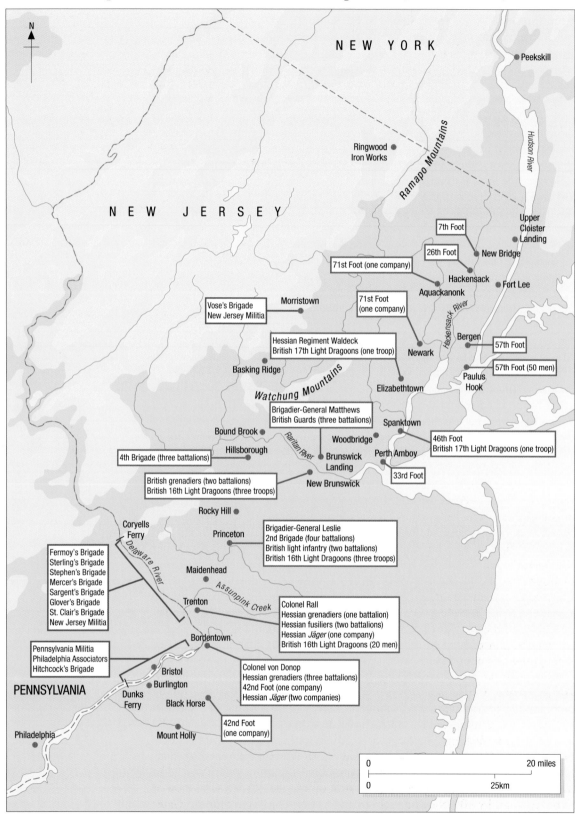

N

NEW YORK

• Peekskill

Ringwood •
Iron Works

NEW JERSEY

Ramapo Mountains

Hudson River

Upper
Cloister
• Landing

7th Foot

26th Foot

New Bridge

71st Foot (one company)

Hackensack
Aquackanonk

Fort Lee

Vose's Brigade
New Jersey Militia

Morristown •

71st Foot
(one company)

Hackensack River

Bergen •

57th Foot

Hessian Regiment Waldeck
British 17th Light Dragoons (one troop)

Newark •

Paulus
Hook

57th Foot (50 men)

Basking Ridge •

Watchung Mountains

Elizabethtown •

Brigadier-General Matthews
British Guards (three battalions)

Spanktown •

Bound Brook •

Raritan River

Woodbridge •

46th Foot
British 17th Light Dragoons (one troop)

4th Brigade (three battalions)

Hillsborough •

Brunswick
Landing

Perth Amboy •

British grenadiers (two battalions)
British 16th Light Dragoons (three troops)

New Brunswick

33rd Foot

Rocky Hill •

Coryells
Ferry

Princeton •

Brigadier-General Leslie
2nd Brigade (four battalions)
British light infantry (two battalions)
British 16th Light Dragoons (three troops)

Fermoy's Brigade
Sterling's Brigade
Stephen's Brigade
Mercer's Brigade
Sargent's Brigade
Glover's Brigade
St. Clair's Brigade
New Jersey Militia

Delaware River

Maidenhead •

Assunpink Creek

Trenton •

Colonel Rall
Hessian grenadiers (one battalion)
Hessian fusiliers (two battalions)
Hessian Jäger (one company)
British 16th Light Dragoons (20 men)

Pennsylvania Militia
Philadelphia Associators
Hitchcock's Brigade

Bordentown •

PENNSYLVANIA

Bristol •
• Burlington

Dunks
Ferry

Black Horse •

Colonel von Donop
Hessian grenadiers (three battalions)
42nd Foot (one company)
Hessian Jäger (two companies)

Philadelphia •

Mount Holly •

42nd Foot
(one company)

0   20 miles

0   25km

Thompson-Neely House, now part of the Washington Crossing Historic Park, was one of several local houses used for medical treatment of sick and convalescing soldiers during the winter of 1776/77. James Monroe, future President, and William Washington recovered from wounds received during the battle of Trenton at the Thompson-Neely House. (Author's collection)

As early as December 13 Washington seems to have begun spinning out the outline of a possible counterattack. Even as he was justifiably reaching the end of patience with Lee's vacillations, Washington wrote to him that day:

> The advantages they have gained over us in the past have made them so proud and sure of success that they have determined to go to Philadelphia this winter. I have positive information that this is a fact that because the term of service of the light troops of Jersey and Maryland are ended they anticipate the weakness of our army. Should they now really risk this undertaking then there is a great probability that they will pay dearly for it and I shall continue to retreat before them so as to lull them into security.

Washington's efforts at collecting information began to pay dividends. By December 15 Washington had information that the British were going into winter quarters. A letter to Connecticut governor Joseph Trumbull, Sr. on December 14 suggested that Washington was already considering the possibility that he was considering to "attempt a stroke upon the Forces of the Enemy, who lay a good deal scattered and to all appearance, in a state of security. A lucky blow in this Quarter would be fatal to them and would most certainly raise the spirits of the People …" To Maj. Gen. Heath he suggested that, "if we can draw our Force speedily, I should hope we may effect something of importance …"

Washington conferred with several of his senior staff at Buckingham throughout this period. Washington wrote to Joseph Reed responding to his suggestion for an attack, requesting "For Heaven's sake keep this to yourself, as discovery of it may prove fatal to us … but necessity, dire necessity, will, nay must, justify an attempt."

Lee's troops, now under the command of Maj. Gen. Sullivan, finally marched into Washington's camp along the Delaware in a snowstorm on December 20. Greatly diminished in numbers, those remaining were without blankets or shoes. Whatever exaggerations Charles Lee had been guilty of he had not overstated the deplorable condition of his men. They were followed two days later by 600 New England troops led by Brig. Gen. Horatio Gates

This is the view that Washington and his men had looking across the Delaware River from McKonkey's Ferry toward New Jersey. On the night of December 25, 1776, the Delaware River would have appeared less pacific, choked with ice and choppy from the rising winds. (Author's collection)

and General Benedict Arnold from Schuyler's Northern Command. Despite Washington's request that he take part in the coming attack Gates begged off and hurried off to find the Congress. Arnold, who would have like nothing better than to be given a command, was dispatched to Rhode Island to stiffen the resistance to General Clinton's expedition.

On December 11 the Congress passed a resolve calling for a day of fasting and humiliation, encouraging the "exercise of repentance and reformation." The next day the same Congress, shaken by the British advance and imminent threat to Philadelphia voted to give Washington "full power to order and direct all things relative ... to the operation of the war" for six months. Although grateful for this authority, Maj. Gen. Greene and others pressed Congress to grant Washington "full Power to take such measures he may find necessary to promote the Establishment of the New Army." On December 27 as the crisis deepened Congress extended Washington's powers.

On December 17 Grant wrote, "I can hardly believe that Washington would venture at this season of the year to pass the Delaware at Vessel's ferry as the repassing it may on account of the ice become difficult."

Although two Hessian engineers drew up plans and recommended to Rall that a redoubt be constructed at the upper end of the town, and Major von Dechow also suggested the construction of fortifications, Rall was contemptuous of the Americans and rejected any suggestion that Trenton be fortified. Compounding Rall's stubborn refusal to listen to advice was the open hostility between Rall and Donop. Neither hid their obvious disdain for each other and, although they were only six miles apart, they communicated infrequently

As soon as Rall's men settled down in Trenton he found himself engaged in a desultory war of attrition. Almost every day saw soldiers ambushed while on patrol or lost while foraging. American militia were active across the New Jersey countryside. Most of these attacks were uncoordinated reactions to the continuing plundering and looting of the locals. Groups of militia engaged in running battles with Hessian and British units. To punctuate the seriousness of the enemy attacks, Rall sent a dispatch to Princeton escorted by 100 men. Rall's gesture only resulted in further derision from skeptical

British officers. Patrols traveling north to Howell's Ferry, a mere four miles away, were regularly attacked by local bands of militia. While the militia attacks produced benefits to the American cause by disrupting enemy communications and gathering useful intelligence, their random nature resulted in an extremely fluid situation that defied Washington's attempts to confirm the exact location of enemy units at any given time.

South of Trenton, Brig. Gen. James Ewing, with 600 militia, launched a series of hit-and-run attacks across the river on December 17 and 18 leaving Rall and the Hessians shaken. On the night of December 21, faces blackened, Ewing's men crossed the Delaware and burned several houses at the ferry landing and vanished. Although the losses of men were slight, these raids began to play on the Hessians' nerves and confidence.

Rumors of an imminent American raid in force resulted in Rall organizing a fruitless march along the Delaware to search for the raiders. Rall deployed his cannon in the center of town, unsure from which direction an attack might come and required his men to sleep in their clothes so that they might be able to respond at a moment's notice. Rall wrote to Donop on December 22 noting sarcastically that Maj. Gen. Grant "has also written me and what makes me pleased is that he knows the strength of the enemy thirty miles off, better than we do here. He writes me the enemy are naked, hungry and very weak …"

Donop's anticipation that the Grenadier Battalion von Köhler and heavy artillery would soon bolster his forces were dashed by Grant on December 17, in a message stating that the grenadiers were still with him and that he should not expect them for some time. Despite his poor estimation of the American fighters Rall began to send increasingly desperate requests for assistance to his superiors. Brigadier-General Leslie at Princeton was sympathetic and responded on December 18 by sending a force of light infantry to Trenton. The overall commander, Maj. Gen. Grant, was far less sympathetic and after receiving three messages from Rall in one day warning of attacks and requesting help, sniffed that Donop should "tell the Colonel he is safe. I will undertake to keep the peace in Jersey with a corporal's guard." Grant also refused Rall's request to garrison troops closer to Trenton at Maidenhead.

On December 22 Washington called a Council of War at Lord Sterling's headquarters to consider an attack against the enemy. He now had all the troops he could reasonably expect for the time being and with the next group of enlistments set to expire on December 31 he needed to act. The day before, Washington's agents had intercepted a letter from a Philadelphia merchant suggesting that the British were waiting only for the Delaware to freeze over before marching to Philadelphia. Included in Washington's gathering was a British spy, probably an aide to one of the American officers. After several hours of inconclusive discussion Washington dismissed the group. The British spy hurried off to report to his patrons. That evening Washington reconvened a smaller, more secure group that drew up the plan to attack Trenton on December 26.

Even as the plans for the attack on Trenton were being formed Washington directed an attack on the enemy around Mt. Holly on December 23. By mid-December Colonel Samuel Griffin had gathered a force of approximately 500 militia, built around an odd collection of Pennsylvania Continentals, in southern New Jersey. On December 14 Griffin's men advanced from Haddonfield toward Mt. Holly. The plan called for Colonel Cadwalader with 700 men to cross the Delaware from Bristol to Burlington early on December 23 to reinforce Griffin. Colonel Joseph Reed was coordinating the movements of the militia units and joined Griffin only to find him sick. Reed returned to Bristol and provided Washington with a summary of what he had seen.

The British also knew about Griffin's men from local Tories. Donop received confirmation on December 21 that Griffin's force was at Mt. Holly. Colonel Sterling, commanding the 42nd Foot at Black Horse, wrote to Donop "… we should not wait to be attacked … You sir, with the troops at Bordentown, should come here and attack. I am confident we are a match for them." On December 23 Donop marched with the 42nd Foot, Grenadier Battalions von Block and von Linsingen, preceded by a detachment of *Jäger*, to Mt. Holly. After driving Griffin's men out of the town Donop settled down to spend the next several days collecting supplies and socializing with a beautiful young widow.

Acting on Reed's pessimistic report from Mt. Holly Washington cancelled the orders for Cadwalader's force to join Griffin but alerted him to stand ready to move to support a larger attack on December 26. Despite the failure of Griffin's raid to inflict serious losses on the enemy it had resulted in Donop's movement south from his headquarters at Bordentown. The result was that Donop's attention was drawn away from the main focus of Washington's attack. Rather than being six miles from Trenton and able to react to an attack on Rall, Donop and his men were a distant 18 miles away on the morning of December 26.

Major-General Grant had received a report from his informer of the discussion of Washington's December 22 war council. He sent a message to Rall, stating that:

> Washington has information that our troops marched into winter quarters and has been told that we are weak at Trenton and Princeton and Lord Sterling expressed a wish to make an attack on these two places. I don't believe he will attempt it, but be assured that my information is undoubtedly true, so I need not advise you to be on your guard …

McKonkey's Ferry Inn provided some shelter for officers of the American Army as they began to cross the Delaware. Local tradition suggests that Washington and his staff ate dinner at the inn early on the evening of December 26, 1776. (Author's collection)

Rall received the note on Christmas Eve. On Christmas Day further information seemed to confirm Grant's warning. Two American deserters told their captors that the American Army was preparing to march.

Rall took what precautions he could. He established six picket outposts, on the Maidenhead, Pennington and River roads, along the road to the Trenton Ferry, at the Assunpink Creek bridge and at the Crosswicks Creek drawbridge. The Crosswicks Creek detachment, positioned four miles south of Trenton, consisted of over 100 men. In case of attack it was instructed to retreat two miles to Bordentown. Within Trenton itself the main picket of 73 men was stationed at the Fox Chase Tavern on the Maidenhead Road. Every night an entire regiment was ordered to remain under arms and all the outposts manned. On Christmas Eve a patrol of over 100 men was sent up the Delaware to Pennington and on Christmas Day the outposts were strengthened. Two hours before daylight a reinforced patrol with two cannon were sent down to the river. Hit and run militia attacks resulted in the entire garrison being called out on December 22, 23 and 25. Despite the increasing

Major-General Israel Putnam commanded American troops on Long Island and in the battles around New York in the summer and early fall of 1776. Putnam was given command of Philadelphia after the American retreat in November and organized militia units to serve with the main army. Putnam failed to cross the Delaware River on the night of December 25, 1776, as Washington had hoped.

activity of the Americans, Rall again rejected the advice of Donop to construct redoubts on the high ground at the head of King and Queen streets and at the Trenton Ferry. In frustration Major von Dechow and Lieutenant-Colonel Scheffer sent a joint letter to General Heister in New York, complaining of Rall's ineptitude.

On Christmas Eve Washington called another council meeting at Greene's headquarters at the Merrick House in Buckingham to work out the details of the attack. Major-generals Greene and Sullivan were joined by brigadier-generals Sterling, Fermoy, Mercer, Stephen and St. Clair. Also attending were colonels Sargent, Stark, Knox and Glover. It was Glover's 14th Massachusetts Continental Regiment that was expected to maneuver the boats taking the army across the Delaware.

One thousand five hundred militia, under Brig. Gen. John Cadwalader and Col. Joseph Reed were ordered to cross the Delaware at Bristol, 12 miles south of Trenton and move toward Burlington. Joining Cadawalader was Hitchcock's Brigade, consisting of roughly 900 men in two Massachusetts and two Rhode Island regiments, assisted by a Rhode Island Militia unit. Major-General Israel Putnam was also expected to bring forward the militia units he had been organizing in Philadelphia to cross the river and act as a reserve.

Seven hundred Pennsylvania Militia, under Brig. Gen. James Ewing, were to cross the river at Trenton to secure the bridge over the Assunpink Creek and prevent a possible Hessian retreat. The main force, with Washington in command, would cross the Delaware at McKonkey's Ferry, nine miles upriver. Once across, this force of 4,000–5,000 men would divide into two columns. One column, led by Maj. Gen. Sullivan would take the River Road into Trenton. Sullivan had Glover's Brigade of five Massachusetts rejiments,

Col. Dudley Sargent's Brigade of two Continental Massachusetts and two Continental New York regiments, along with two Connecticut State regiments. Sullivan's Reserve Brigade, under the command of Brig. Gen. Arthur St. Clair, included four Continental regiments.

The other column, under Maj. Gen Greene, would move inland along the Pennington Road. Greene's force would include Brig. Gen. Adam Stephen's Brigade of three Virginia Continental regiments, Brig. Gen. Hugh Mercer's Brigade of two Massachusetts and two Connecticut Continental regiments, supported by a Connecticut State Regiment, 1st Maryland Continental Regiment and the Maryland/Virginia Rifle Regiment. Lord Sterling's Brigade of two Virginia regiments, the 6th Maryland and Haslett's Delaware Regiment completed the group. A brigade under a French volunteer, Matthias-Alexis Chevalier de la Roche Fermoy was assigned to march behind Greene's force and block any British attempt to reinforce Trenton from the garrison at Princeton.

Four cannon were assigned to each column and Stephen's advance guard included men equipped with hammers, spikes and ropes. These men were either to drag off or spike the Hessian artillery Washington anticipated capturing. Washington, who would accompany Greene's force, emphasized that security was paramount and directed that "a profound silence to be enjoyn'd and no man to quit his Ranks on the pain of Death."

TEN DAYS THAT SHOCKED THE WORLD, DECEMBER 25, 1776, TO JANUARY 3, 1777

The plan called for the main force to cross the Delaware beginning at nightfall on December 25 and march to Trenton, arriving no later than 5.00am. The main attack was scheduled for an hour before dawn, approximately 6.00am. The best guess Washington had of enemy strength at Trenton ranged from 2,000 to 3,000 but he had no guarantee that the militia attacks that plagued the Hessians for the past several weeks might not result in Trenton being reinforced from Donop's command at Bordentown or Leslie's at Princeton without warning.

On December 24 Washington met with Col. Reed and Congressman Dr. Benjamin Rush. Rush later reported that Washington was "much depressed." As they talked about the dim prospects for success Washington scribbled on scraps of paper, dropping them to the ground. After the meeting Reed collected the scraps and found Washington had written a stark but direct phrase, victory or death. This was the password for the night of December 25–26.

December 25, 1776

The plan Washington adopted was complicated and to be completely successful required close coordination and timing. Coordinating the crossing of a major river at three separate places in pitch darkness during a violent storm and attacking Trenton in unison was doomed from the start.

Evidence that things would not go as planned came first with word early on December 25 that Maj. Gen. Putnam would not be able to support the attack with the Philadelphia Militia. Troubling as that was, on Christmas Day the weather took a turn for the worse. Cold and clear all day, the temperature began to rise towards nightfall and it began to rain, followed by hail and then snow, all driven by a howling wind. A northeaster storm was brewing and with it dangerous ice floes in the Delaware.

On Christmas day, contrary to popular myth, there was no celebrating by the Hessian garrison. Early in the day Major von Dechow suggested sending away the baggage which would only hinder the quick deployment of the troops. Rall rejected Dechow's proposal, declaring "These clod-hoppers will not attack us and should they do so, we will simply fall on them and rout them." Rall made his rounds as usual in the later afternoon and retired to the home of Stacy Potts for a game of checkers in the early evening.

About dusk a small group of Americans attacked the picket post on the Pennington Road, wounding six men. Lieutenant-Colonel Brethauer, inspector of the guard, brought up reinforcements and directed a 30-man patrol to push up the Pennington Road after the attackers. By the time that Rall arrived at the head of several companies, the patrol had returned, reporting no contact after marching two miles up the road. After reinforcing the Pennington Road picket, Rall and the Hessians returned to their quarters. Rall told Major von Dechow that this was probably the enemy force that Grant had warned him about. Dechow suggested sending reinforced patrols out along the roads and down to the ferry landings. Rall rejected the suggestion, took no additional precautionary measures and spent the remainder of the evening playing cards at the house of Abraham Hunt, at the corner of Second and King streets.

As the winter storm blew into Trenton the Hessians relaxed. The heavy weather convinced everyone that the Americans would not venture to attack. Despite his concerns over the attack of the previous evening Major von Dechow canceled the standard pre-dawn patrol to the river in light of the raw weather. Rather than their usual 30-man patrol to Johnson's Ferry along the River Road the *Jäger* dispatched a three-man patrol only partway up the river. They reported no enemy contact.

This 19th-century illustration representing Washington's crossing includes well-uniformed American troops struggling against the elements to land boats outfitted with sails. American troops were unevenly dressed and poles rather than sails propelled the boats used to cross.

On the other side of the Delaware, American troops, with 60 rounds of ammunition, three days' worth of rations and a white piece of paper stuck in their hats, began trudging down to the river. One of Washington's aides described the scene, "It is fearfully cold and raw and a snowstorm settling in. The wind is northeast and beats in the faces of the men. It will be a terrible night for the soldiers who have no shoes. Some of them have tied old rags around their feet; others are barefoot, but I have not heard a man complain." At 4.35pm the sun set and the loading began.

Washington's men were to cross the river in a combination of regular ferry craft and special Durham boats. Originally designed by Robert Durham around 1750, these boats were designed to transfer iron ore from the Durham furnaces at Riegelsville to Philadelphia. Later they were used to carry other cargo and could accommodate 15–20 tons per boat. They measured up to 60ft long, had an eight-foot beam and drew only 30in. of water when fully loaded. They had a crew of five, two men with 18ft sweeps on the walking rails on either side and a helmsmen at rear. Each boat carried 50–60 men.

The effects of the building storm, ice floes, swift currents and inevitable confusion in the darkness all contributed to the transfer of troops and equipment falling behind schedule. Glover's Marblehead Regiment, although unfamiliar with the Durham boats, were able to transfer 4,000 men with 18 guns and crews across without incident, though seriously behind schedule. Glover's men were assisted by artillerymen with nautical experience from Captain Joseph Moulder's Company and other local ferrymen. Washington and Knox, who was given overall command of the crossing, were in the first groups to cross. As the Durham boats and regular ferry boats struggled through the ice Washington broke the tension by telling the rotund Knox, who was to supervise the operation, to shift his weight to trim the boat.

Stephen's Brigade was the first over and set up a perimeter of sentries intended to safeguard the landing of those following. By midnight it was clear that the adopted schedule could not be met and, rather than marching the nine miles to Trenton by dawn, it would be much later when they finally reached their destination. While Glover's men got the American infantry over by approximately 2.00am, the transfer of the artillery was a much more difficult challenge and was not completed until after 3.00am. Once the men and guns were sorted out and made ready for the march it was close to

ABOVE
In addition to the Durham boats used to ferry the infantry across the Delaware River, Washington also used regular ferry boats. These shallow craft, which allowed loading from either end, accommodated horses, artillery and wagons for transport across the river. (Author's collection)

LEFT
The Crossing, December 1776 by Lloyd Garrison. This painting provides a more realistic representation of the conditions under which Gen. Washington crossed the Delaware on December 25, 1776. Washington would have used the ferry boat rather than the Durham boat in order to accommodate his horse. Colonel Knox is shown seated beside him and the McKonkey's Ferry Inn can be seen on the Pennsylvania shore. A Durham boat is also shown crossing the river in the distance. (Provided by Swan Historical Foundation, National Museum of the American Revolution)

4.00am. In the meantime the men built fires to warm themselves while Washington and his staff sought shelter in the ferry house.

Washington had already been notified by Col. Reed that the planned crossing of Cadawalader's men near Bristol was not going well. He now realized that his intention to attack Trenton at daybreak was unrealistic. Aides described Washington, wrapped in his cloak, supervising the landings as, "calm and collected, but very determined." Washington would later write that "I was certain there was no making a retreat without being discovered and harassed on repassing the river. I was determined to push on at all events."

With the timetable for the attack now in shambles Washington also had to contend with the possibility that Brig. Gen. Ewing's planned crossing

Colonel Henry Knox, commander of American artillery, was given responsibility by Washington for overseeing the crossing on December 25, 1776. Knox accompanied Washington in crossing the Delaware early in the evening.

directly into Trenton would alert the garrison. Here the weather worked to the American advantage as Ewing's militiamen failed utterly in crossing the 1,000ft-wide river.

Further south, Cadwalader's militia, which included approximately 130 Marines under the command of Major Samuel Nicholas and Colonel Daniel Hitchcock's New England Continentals, considered their options. Rather than cross from Bristol to Burlington, which was under enemy surveillance, Cadwalader decided to march several miles further south and cross at Dunk's Ferry. Unfortunately the Delaware, nearly 1,200ft wide at this point, was even more choked with ice floes. The ice formed a barrier 150ft from the New Jersey shore and it was with great difficulty that the first wave of infantry was able to cross. As the storm increased in strength, so did the ice floes and it became more difficult to maneuver the boats. When it became clear that the artillery would not be able to land, Cadwalader ordered the operation cancelled and recalled the troops already in New Jersey. Washington would have to defeat the Trenton garrison alone.

With his force now assembled Washington and his bodyguard, 21 men of the 1st Troop of Philadelphia Light Horse, led the mile-long column along a sloping, wooded track away from the river, into the teeth of the intensifying storm. One-and-a-half miles from the Delaware the column turned southeast, putting the driving wind, rain, sleet and snow at their back. After marching for some distance on relatively flat country the column reached Jacob's Creek, 100ft down a rutted path. The steep decline, coupled with the ice and snow, required the artillery to be unhitched, slowly lowered down the path, across the swiftly flowing stream and then dragged up the opposite back, taking more precious time. After passing Jacob's Creek the column, now exposed to the fury of the northeaster, the Americans made their way down the sloping road to the Birmingham Crossroads.

It was now 6.30am and dawn was not far away. With his staff gathered around him Washington reaffirmed his plan to dispatch Greene's force along the Upper Ferry Road to the Scotch Road and then to the Pennington Road. Sullivan's men were to continue along the River Road and enter Trenton at Water Street. Close coordination of the attacks of the two columns was critical and a bystander noted that "the General gave orders that every officer's watch should be set by his and the movements of the attack fixed." When notified that the men's flints and ammunition were wet and unusable Washington responded simply, "advance and charge."

Having a longer march Greene's column set out first led by Stephen's Brigade, followed by Mercer, Fermoy and Lord Sterling. The columns marched accompanied by blazing torches attached to the artillery carriages. Washington watched his men struggle forward and in a deep, solemn voice encouraged them "Soldiers, keep by your officers. For God's sake, keep by your officers."

Major-General Sullivan's column was given a short rest and then started out led by Colonel Stark's 5th New Hampshire Regiment, followed by Col. Glover's Brigade, Brig. Gen. St. Clair's Brigade and Col. Sargent's men. Knox's artillery was distributed between the two columns.

Advance guards preceded each column on their march to Trenton. Captain John Flahaven of the 1st New Jersey Continentals led Sullivan's column. Captain William Washington, a distant cousin of the commander-in-chief led Greene's force. His assistant was 18-year-old Lieutenant James Monroe.

At about 7.30am, as they approached Trenton, Greene's men were surprised by a force of about 40 American militia, marching away from the town. Washington learned that the group, led by Captain George Wallis, were members of the 4th Virginia Regiment and had attacked the Hessian picket on Pennington Road. They had been dispatched the day before by Brig. Gen. Stephen, who was then unaware of Washington's plans, to attack the Hessians in revenge for the death of one of their members. They had crossed on Christmas Eve and managed to attack the Hessian outpost on Christmas night, wounding several of the enemy. Washington, who interrogated Wallis, was mortified and turned on Stephen, chastising him for endangering the whole enterprise by his unauthorized act. Regaining his composure Washington directed Wallis's group to join the advance guard.

Just before 8.00am Greene's column reached the northern edge of Trenton, approximately one mile from the center of town. Screened by a crop of woods Greene organized his three brigades, arranging Mercer's Brigade on the right, Sterling's Brigade in the center and Fermoy's men on the left. Stephen's Virginians were to lead the assault. Colonel Charles Scott deployed his 5th Virginia Regiment and gave them final instructions. "Take care now and fire low. Bring down your pieces. Fire at their legs. One man wounded in the leg is better than a dead one for it takes two more to carry him off and there is three gone. Leg them, damn 'em. I say, leg them!"

In a thick snow squall Greene's columns pushed through the woods and engaged the Hessian post at Howell's cooper shop, near the intersection of Scotch Road and Pennington Road. Stephen's Virginians pushed back the Hessian outposts as they rushed into Trenton from the north. Recognizing that they were in danger of being enveloped the main Hessian detachment fell back, engaged in a running skirmish and losing several men. Fermoy's Brigade, composed of riflemen from Col. Edward Hand's 1st Pennsylvania Regiment and Col. Nicholas Haussegger's Pennsylvania German Regiment, moved toward the Princeton Road and pushed back the Hessian outpost. Both detachments retired to the head of King and Queen streets, where they were joined by a detachment from the Fusilier Regiment von Lossberg. Together they tried to stem the American onslaught but were soon forced back into the village, using the houses and outbuildings for cover.

Johnson Ferry House is located on the New Jersey side of the Delaware. Washington and staff took refuge from the storm as the crossing dragged on through the night. (Author's collection)

ABOVE
The terrain on the Pennsylvania bank of the Delaware was relatively flat, allowing for the efficient deployment of the American Army as it waited to cross. The New Jersey bank was much more steep, requiring American troops to struggle to march up to level ground. (Author's collection)

RIGHT
Fireplace in the Johnson Ferry House. Washington and his staff warmed themselves in this room as they waited. (Author's collection)

Sullivan's column also approached Trenton just before 8.00am. Flahaven's advance guard, along with the 1st New Hampshire Regiment moved quickly against a small house used by Hessian pickets and the *Jäger* company deployed at the Hermitage. After driving off the pickets, Sullivan's men pushed the *Jäger* back toward the barracks on Front Street. The *Jäger* fired several volleys at their pursuers before retreating toward the stone bridge over the Assunpink Creek. Stark's New Hampshire Regiment pushed ahead, leading the column into Trenton.

American artillery, deployed opposite Trenton on the west bank of the Delaware, also began to bombard the village adding to the Hessian

discomfort. The bombardment was hampered by the range of nearly 600 yards, poor visibility because of the storm and, most importantly, limited ability to distinguish between friend and foe once the Americans advanced into the village and engaged the Hessians at close quarters.

With the Hessians retreating into Trenton, Greene's artillery deployed on the high ground at the head of King and Queen streets. Captain Thomas Forrest deployed his two 6-pdr guns and two 5.5in. howitzers to fire down Queen Street, and was joined by Hamilton's two 6-pdr guns, which commanded King Street. Together the six pieces fired down the two streets into the center of Trenton. Brigadier-General Mercer's Brigade infiltrated along the west side of King Street, occupying houses and taking refuge between the buildings. On the left Greene directed Captain Baumann to bring up his 3-pdr guns.

Rall, awakened by his adjutant, Lieutenant Jacob Piel, directed the Fusilier Regiment von Lossberg to form behind the graveyard of the English Church, before riding down King Street toward his own regiment. The Grenadier Regiment Rall, commanded by Lieutenant-Colonel Balthasar Brethauer, mustered on King Street north of Second Street. They advanced up King Street and were met with a storm of shot and shell from the American artillery to their front and on their left flank from elements of Mercer's men. At the lower end of Queen Street the Fusilier Regiment von Knyphausen formed up.

Mercer's Brigade, advancing down the west side of King Street, occupied Pott's Tannery along Petty's Run and took Rall's men under fire from their left. Rall's two-gun artillery section moved in advance of the regiment up King Street, over a branch of Petty's Run and deployed under intense fire

Opening of the Battle of Trenton by William E. Pedrick showing Washington watching as his men struggle to deploy in the sleet and snow at Trenton. (Courtesy of the Old Barracks Association, Trenton, NJ)

from American artillery and Mercer's men. The guns fired several rounds before many of the crew and horse were killed or wounded.

As he deployed his men Rall spoke to Lieutenant Andreas von Wiederholdt, who had commanded the Hessian outpost along the Pennington Road. Wiederholdt erroneously reported that the Americans had surrounded Trenton, leading Rall to believe he had no choice but to attempt to break out of the trap. In reality, at this point Rall could have led his men south and retired across the bridge over the Assunpink Creek to more defensible ground on the south bank.

Washington, accompanied by the Philadelphia Light Horse, watched the attack unfold from the high ground at the intersection of King and Queen streets. From his vantage point Washington could see Sullivan's men advance along the river, Mercer's men attacking King Street and Stephen's and Fermoy's commands deploying on the eastern edge of Trenton. Visibility was still limited by the storm, which continued in intensity, and the buildings of the village. There were numerous houses and outbuildings along King Street, restricting the field of fire of the artillery and offering cover to both sides. Queen Street, with fewer houses, offered a more open view

Rall ordered his regiment and the Fusilier Regiment von Lossberg to advance up King Street toward the American batteries. The Grenadier Regiment Rall moved up to the small bridge over Petty's Run in support of the Hessian artillery and fired two volleys before being scattered by fire from the American artillery. Portions of the regiment re-formed with Col. Rall, while others fled down Queen Street, some joining the Fusilier Regiment von Knyphausen while others retreated across the Assunpink Creek.

Sterling's Brigade, forming the center of Greene's line, advanced down King and Queen streets. Captain Washington and Lieutenant Monroe leading the small unit equipped with ropes and spiking equipment rushed to seize the

Hessian guns. Hessian artillerymen tried unsuccessfully to defend the cannon and Rall directed a group of grenadiers to support the artillery. After a short fight, in which both Washington and Monroe were wounded, the Americans captured the artillery.

Mercer's Brigade took up positions behind fences and in the buildings along King and Queen streets, and kept the Fusilier Regiment von Lossberg under a harassing fire. Scattered elements of Grenadier Regiment Rall, including the color guard, joined the Fusilier Regiment von Lossberg and together they retreated to the east across Queen Street. Still under fire the Fusilier Regiment von Lossberg and refugees from the Grenadier Regiment Rall, retired beyond Queen Street toward Dark Lane, accompanied by Colonel Rall.

At the foot of Queen Street, artillerymen from the Fusilier Regiment von Knyphausen advanced two guns up the street to guard against an American assault. They engaged the American artillery briefly before one gun was disabled. The other gun was brought forward to support the counterattack of the Grenadier Regiment Rall and Fusilier Regiment von Lossberg.

As the fight raged in the center of Trenton, Sullivan's Division pushed along the Delaware River and advanced to the east along Second Street. The Fusilier Regiment von Knyphausen, deployed along Queen Street and extending on both sides of Second Street, detached a company at Second Street to protect their line of retreat to the Assunpink Creek, while the remaining four companies advanced a far as King Street. Colonel John Stark's New Hampshire Regiment, with Captain Moulder's three 4-pdr guns, deployed to engage the Fusilier Regiment von Knyphausen near the Bull Head Tavern.

Colonel Sargent's Brigade and Col. Glover's Brigade, accompanied by Captain Daniel Neil's and Captain Winthrop Sargent's companies, moved down Front Street to secure the bridge over the Assunpink Creek. Glover's

The barracks at Trenton, New Jersey, were built in 1757 to house troops participating in the French and Indian War. Both American and British forces used it during the Revolution. On December 26, 1776, Hessian *Jäger* briefly defended the barracks before retreating. (Author's collection)

BRITISH FORCES
A Fusilier Regiment von Lossberg
B Grenadier Regiment Rall
C Fusilier Regiment von Knyphausen
D Rall 3-pdr guns
E Knyphausen 3-pdr guns
F Lossberg 3-pdr guns

(SEE MAP PAGE 58)

The battle of Trenton

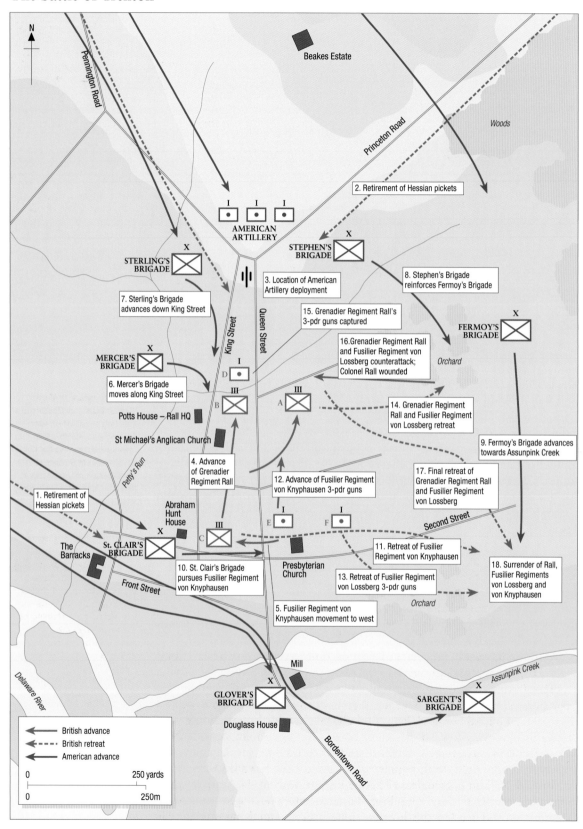

Beakes Estate

Pennington Road

Princeton Road

Woods

2. Retirement of Hessian pickets

AMERICAN ARTILLERY

STERLING'S BRIGADE

STEPHEN'S BRIGADE

8. Stephen's Brigade reinforces Fermoy's Brigade

7. Sterling's Brigade advances down King Street

3. Location of American Artillery deployment

15. Grenadier Regiment Rall's 3-pdr guns captured

FERMOY'S BRIGADE

MERCER'S BRIGADE

King Street

Queen Street

16. Grenadier Regiment Rall and Fusilier Regiment von Lossberg counterattack; Colonel Rall wounded

Orchard

6. Mercer's Brigade moves along King Street

Potts House – Rall HQ

St Michael's Anglican Church

Petty's Run

14. Grenadier Regiment Rall and Fusilier Regiment von Lossberg retreat

9. Fermoy's Brigade advances towards Assunpink Creek

4. Advance of Grenadier Regiment Rall

12. Advance of Fusilier Regiment von Knyphausen 3-pdr guns

17. Final retreat of Grenadier Regiment Rall and Fusilier Regiment von Lossberg

1. Retirement of Hessian pickets

Abraham Hunt House

Second Street

The Barracks

St. CLAIR'S BRIGADE

11. Retreat of Fusilier Regiment von Knyphausen

18. Surrender of Rall, Fusilier Regiments von Lossberg and von Knyphausen

10. St. Clair's Brigade pursues Fusilier Regiment von Knyphausen

Front Street

Presbyterian Church

13. Retreat of Fusilier Regiment von Lossberg 3-pdr guns

Orchard

5. Fusilier Regiment von Knyphausen movement to west

Delaware River

Mill

Assunpink Creek

GLOVER'S BRIGADE

SARGENT'S BRIGADE

Douglass House

British advance
British retreat
American advance

0   250 yards

0   250m

Bordentown Road

58

men crossed the creek and occupied the high ground on the south bank. Rall's only escape route was now sealed.

The Fusilier Regiment von Lossberg and Grenadier Regiment Rall reorganized northeast of the village, along low ground near an apple orchard. Beyond the orchard Fermoy's Brigade occupied the high ground denying Rall any hope of retiring toward the Princeton Road. The remnants of Grenadier Regiment Rall retrieved their colors and, with the Fusilier Regiment von Lossberg on the right, both regiments advanced back toward Queen Street led by Col. Rall on horseback. The American artillery at the head of Queen Street, supported by Sterling's Brigade, fired into their right flank while Mercer's men defended the houses along Queen and King streets. The

The Trenton Battle Monument, completed in 1893 and made of granite, is located at the approximate spot where American artillery deployed in support of the attack. A statue of George Washington tops the monument, arm outstretched toward Trenton. (Author's collection)

Hessians advanced toward Church Alley and Queen Street but their attack stalled and Col. Rall was wounded. Exposed to the snow and wind the Hessians found it difficult to fire at the enemy who were protected in the houses and buildings.

Further to the south the Fusilier Regiment von Knyphausen engaged in a firefight with St. Clair's Brigade at Second Street and King Street. Noting that men from Sterling's Brigade were moving down King Street on their right flank the Fusilier Regiment von Knyphausen retired to Queen Street where refugees from Grenadier Regiment Rall and some of the artillery crews joined them. As the Fusilier Regiment von Knyphausen retreated further east, St. Clair's Brigade advanced. Captain Moulder's Company deployed at Second and Queen Street, firing into Rall's group from their left.

Colonel Rall, thinking that retreat over the Assunpink Creek might be possible, sent an aide toward the bridge, only to be told the Americans blocked that route. Rall then ordered a general retreat back to the apple orchard. After issuing the order Rall was again wounded, receiving two musket balls in his body and falling from his horse. Lieutenant-Colonel Scheffer, now in command, directed the Hessians back to the orchard. After holding a brief council with the remaining officers they all agreed to attempt to break out toward the Princeton Road. They advanced a short distance to the east but were stopped by Fermoy's and Stephen's brigades blocking their route.

Major Freidrich Ludwig von Dechow led the Fusilier Regiment von Knyphausen and stragglers from the Rall and Lossberg regiments to a small orchard just north of the Assunpink Creek. Dechow, who was wounded in the hip during the retreat, initially determined to push his way across the Assunpink Creek but found men from Sargent's Brigade deployed to defend the bridge. Glover's Brigade and Captain Sargent's Company commanded the high ground on the south bank of the Creek. Dechow initially ordered his men to attempt to ford the creek and escape as best they could. Two guns from the Fusilier Regiment von Lossberg accompanied the Fusilier Regiment von Knyphausen and these became mired in the swampy ground near the creek, causing valuable time to be lost in an unsuccessful attempt to free them. Now discouraged, Dechow rejected suggestions that the regiment attempt to escape and resolved to surrender. Assisted by an aide Dechow hobbled to the corner of Queen and Front streets where he offered his sword to Maj. Gen. Sullivan. Dechow would later die from his wounds.

While Dechow surrendered to Sullivan the noose around the bulk of the Fusilier Regiment von Knyphausen tightened. Small groups of officers and men did succeed in crossing the Assunpink Creek but after Brig. Gen. St. Clair issued a blunt warning that further resistance would result in the destruction of the remaining men the Hessians gave up.

Further north the Grenadier Regiment Rall and Fusilier Regiment von Lossberg , now surrounded by American troops, also surrendered. Despite their attempts to seal the bridge over the Assunpink Creek approximately 350 men escaped, including an assortment of outposts and refugees from all three Hessian regiments, artillerymen, *Jäger* and a 20-man detachment of British light dragoons. Most of the men retired toward Bordentown, where they reported news of the disaster to Colonel von Minnigerode. A small group from the Fusilier Regiment von Knyphausen struck out to the east and arrived in Princeton at 8.00pm. Brigadier-General Leslie quickly dispatched messages to Major-General Grant at New Brunswick, who in turn alerted General Howe in New York.

Trenton, 26 December, 1776 by H. Charles McBarron. McBarron captures the moment when American infantry moved down King Street to overrun the Grenadier Regiment Rall's two-gun company. McBarron accurately represents the ragged condition of American troops. (US Army Center of Military History)

In Trenton the Americans herded their captives into the center of the village and collected the spoils of victory. Colonel Rall, fatally wounded, was carried to his headquarters, the Potts House. Generals Washington and Greene stopped briefly and talked to Rall about the disposition of the Hessian prisoners. Rall died on the evening of December 27 and was buried in an unmarked grave in the Presbyterian churchyard on Second Street.

American losses were slight, four wounded and four killed, although many others suffered long-term disabilities from exposure and exhaustion. Hessian losses amounted to 22 killed, 83 seriously wounded and approximately 900 captured. Numerous supplies, including three ammunition wagons, 12 drums and six brass guns were also taken.

With the victory won Washington was faced with another decision. Should he follow up on this success and strike at either Bordentown or Princeton? The opinion of his officers was split with Greene and Knox in favor of pursuing their advantage while others urged caution, particularly in light of the physical condition of the men and the continuing storm. By this time Washington was also aware that neither Cadwalader nor Ewing had crossed the river to support his attack. Mitigating against further action was news that his men had availed themselves of 40 hogsheads of rum. Washington gave the order for retreat and prepared a note to John Hancock, describing the victory and outlining his reasons for retreat.

The main body of Washington's army retraced their steps to McKonkey's Ferry for the trip back across the Delaware with prisoners and supplies. To speed up the process, some men and officers re-crossed over the Trenton Ferry, Beatty's Ferry and Johnson's Ferry. The snow now changed to rain, making conditions even more miserable for all. Ice floes continued to restrict access to both shores and men were forced to wade into the freezing water to enter and exit the boats. The Philadelphia Light Horse remained on the New Jersey side until nightfall, patrolling the roads leading to the ferry crossing.

A 19th-century view of the Hessian surrender, inaccurately showing Hessian troops surrendering in formation in front of their tents, amid a landscape devoid of any hint of the village of Trenton.

Interlude

News of the American victory spread quickly. The overall impact was summed up by Admiral Howe's private secretary, Ambrose Serle, who wrote on December 27, "Heard the unpleasant news of a whole Brigade of Hessians under Col. Rall being taken Prisoners at Trenton by a large body of Rebels and at nine o'clock in the morning. I was exceedingly concerned on the public account, as it will tend to revive the drooping spirits of the rebels and increase their force."

Recriminations began almost immediately. The British high command blamed the Hessians for their laxity, while Hessian officers pointed to Howe's flawed troop dispositions in New Jersey as the reason for the calamity. Meanwhile Donop, hearing the news in Mt. Holly, resolved to retreat, marching first to Allentown and then to Princeton. Howe responded to the news by writing Grant that he was sending Lt. Gen. Cornwallis, who had not yet sailed to England, to consult with Grant and extended a "Merry Christmas to you notwithstanding all our disasters." Grant wrote Donop contemptuously "if I was with you, your Grenadiers and Yagers, I should not be afraid of an attack from Washington's Army, which is almost naked and does not exceed 8,000 men."

With the army headquarters established at Newtown, five miles from the river, Washington again considered his options. After dispatching a lengthy description of the battle and the captured flags to Congress, on the afternoon of December 27 Washington received word from Brig. Gen. Cadwalader that he had crossed over to New Jersey with 1,800 men, including Hitchcock's Brigade and the Philadelphia Associators. Cadwalader reported the enemy had retreated in some haste to the east and rumors of panic were rampant. After encouraging Washington to return to New Jersey with the main army he told Washington that he would retire to Burlington and await further orders.

Recognizing another opportunity Washington assembled a war council later that evening. After laying out the options Washington let the council prepare a recommendation. The council found the potential advantages of dealing the British another defeat outweighed the risks. Washington, who favored a resumption of the campaign, sent messages to militia commanders in northern and western New Jersey and eastern Pennsylvania, informing them of his plans and encouraging them to call out their men. More problematic was keeping the Continentals whose terms of enlistment ran out at the end of the year. With these considerations in mind Washington dispatched Brig. Gen. Thomas Mifflin to take overall command of Cadwalader's mixed force.

Washington planned on a much larger operation, using eight crossing points to get the army over quickly. The unpredictable winter weather continued to cause problems. On December 28 a storm left up to six inches of snow throughout the Delaware Valley before the air turned frigid. Ice began forming along the Delaware River during the night and, as Washington's men began their crossing early on December 29, sections of the Delaware River were covered with ice. The pace of crossing was torturous. Some of Greene's infantry were able to walk gingerly across the ice at Yarkley's Ferry but the artillery and supplies were stranded on the Pennsylvania side. Further up the river, Sullivan's Division was unable to cross at all. The next morning they tried again and spent the day struggling to complete the crossing.

On December 27, even before they had received word of the triumph at Trenton, the Continental Congress passed a resolution vesting extraordinary powers in Washington in response to the ongoing crisis. They authorized Washington, for a six-month period, to raise additional units of infantry, cavalry and artillery, appoint all officers up to the rank of brigadier-general, to seize property and goods if necessary and imprison any citizen deemed to harbor loyalist sympathies.

Cadwalader's arrival in New Jersey was also reported to Col. von Donop in Allentown early on December 28, along with rumors that after combining with the New Jersey Militia Cadwalader intended to attack Princeton. On his own initiative Donop resolved to march to Princeton, an action immediately confirmed by a letter from Grant, who, despite his earlier

This 19th-century illustration fancifully shows Washington leading the advance against the Hessians at Trenton. In reality Washington watched the battle unfold at the head of King and Queen streets where the three American batteries were deployed.

Washington Receiving a Salute on the Field of Trenton represents another 19th-century attempt to capture the spirit of Washington's victory at Trenton. This illustration shows a heroic, albeit older Washington astride a white horse recognizing the salute.

bravado, appears to have become concerned about another attack. Brigadier-General Leslie was ordered by Grant to throw out patrols towards Trenton to cover Donop's march. Donop's Brigade arrived in Princeton in the mid-afternoon of December 28.

Rumors of the appearance of Washington's army were rife, resulting in frantic marches and counter marches. Concerned about a possible attack from the direction of Trenton, and to ease the overcrowding at Princeton, Brig. Gen. Leslie dispatched the British light infantry to Maidenhead and the 42nd Foot to Stony Creek. Colonel Block was assigned to defend Kingston. The next day Leslie redeployed the 42nd Foot to Maidenhead to support the light infantry and the Lingsingen Regiment was stationed at Stony Brook.

Cadwalader left Burlington early on December 29 and occupied Bordentown that afternoon. Small patrols and raiding parties were sent out to search for the enemy. On the same day Brig. Gen. Mifflin arrived in Bordentown after taking command of over 1,500 additional Pennsylvania militia at Bristol the day before. Mifflin then addressed Hitchcock's Brigade, composed of New England Continentals, four miles away at Crosswicks on December 30. Mifflin made an impassioned appeal to the New Englanders to stay on past the end of their enlistment, promising an additional bounty.

Although Mifflin was successful in convincing the majority of Hitchcock's men to stay on, Washington was having mixed results with the rest of the army. Most conspicuous was the decision of Glover's 14th Massachusetts Regiment to return to Boston rather than extend their service. Colonel John Haslett's 1st Delaware Regiment, reduced to just 92 men from their original strength of 750 six months earlier, also rejected calls to remain under arms. While the army was still struggling to get over the Delaware River Washington paraded the Continental units in Trenton and addressed them:

> My brave fellows, you have done all I have asked you to do, and more than could be reasonably expected. But your country is at stake, your wives, your houses and all that you hold dear. You have worn yourself out with fatigues and hardships, but we know not how to spare you. If you will consent to stay only one month longer, you will render service to the cause of liberty and to your country which you probably never can do under any other circumstances. The present is emphatically the crisis which is to decide our destiny.

Through this desperate appeal and a ten dollar bounty, equal to about six weeks' work, Washington was able to induce approximately 1,400 men of the three New England brigades, Glover's, Sargent's and St. Clair's, to remain with the army for the next six weeks. Mercer's and Sterling's commands were down to a combined 325 men. With Stephen's Virginia troops and Fermoy's Pennsylvanians, Washington could call on about 3,300 veteran troops.

Compensating for the loss of the Continental troops, militia were flocking to the colors. Before joining Cadwalader, Brig. Gen. Mifflin had assumed command of a brigade made up of elements of five new Pennsylvania

Continental regiments, portions of numerous Pennsylvania militia regiments and Major Thomas Proctor's two-gun company.

Washington, desperate to determine the strength of Cornwallis and his direction of approach, dispatched Col. Joseph Reed and 12 militia cavalry to gather intelligence. About three miles from Princeton, Reed and his party discovered a forage party of British light dragoons and took them captive. From the prisoners Washington was given credible information on the size of Cornwallis's force and their intention to attack him at Trenton. About the same time Cadwalader told Washington he had a spy who had collected information on the Princeton garrison determining that they were deployed on the western edge of town, leaving the eastern approaches open. Cadwalader provided a rough map showing a back road used occasionally by local farmers, leading to this area.

At his temporary headquarters on Queen Street near the Assunpink Bridge Washington convened a council with his senior staff on December 30. He updated his staff on the latest intelligence and reviewed options. Washington rejected any suggestion that the army retreat back to Pennsylvania. There was general agreement that they should offer battle at Trenton. Once again the Americans were faced with a difficult decision. The British had recovered from their paralysis more quickly than anticipated. Coupled with the delays in re-crossing the Delaware River, the continuing effort to cajole enough veterans to stay with the army, the ongoing assembly of various militia units and lack of concrete knowledge of British intentions, the overall situation was shifting dramatically.

Cadwalader had sent a detachment as far as Cranbury on December 30 based on intelligence that Cornwallis had left a skeleton force of only 250 men at New Brunswick. Cadwalader's orders were to overwhelm the New Brunswick garrison, rescue Maj. Gen. Lee and secure the £70,000 military treasury. Late on December 30 Cadwalader learned that the New Brunswick garrison totaled 1,500 and he reluctantly ordered his men back to Allentown.

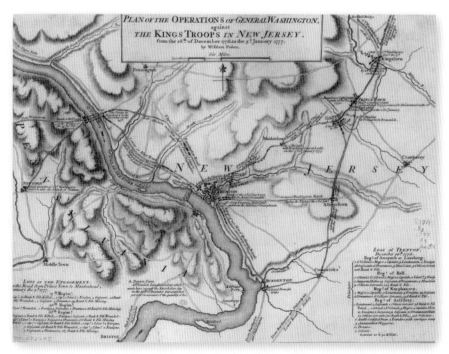

Operations of General Washington against the King's Troops in New Jersey. This map shows the various movements of both American and British forces between December 25, 1776, and January 3, 1777, and the relative locations of Trenton, Princeton and Bordentown.

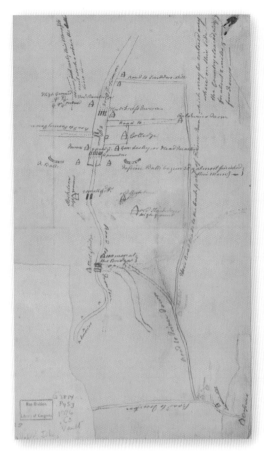

With the addition of Cadwalader's and Mifflin's men Washington's force totaled approximately 6,800 men and nearly 30 guns. His army occupied good defensive ground, a ridgeline commanding a creek swollen by recent rains and crossed by only one bridge. Washington suspected that the British and their Hessian allies would be eager to redeem themselves after their defeat at Trenton and precipitous flight to Princeton. He may have hoped that in their reckless pursuit they could be enticed to shatter themselves on the strong American defenses along the ridge south of the Assunpink. Washington also knew his position had serious flaws. While his left flank was anchored on the Delaware his right flank was vulnerable, hanging in the air.

On December 31 Washington directed Fermoy's Brigade, including Col. Hand's 1st Pennsylvania Regiment and Col. Haussegger's Pennsylvania German Regiment, augmented by Stephen's Brigade, now commanded by Colonel Charles Scott, and Captain Forrest's Company to take up positions just south of Maidenhead and delay the British advance. The American riflemen advanced further north to Little Shabakunk Creek.

On January 1, 1777, Maj. Gen. Grant marched from New Brunswick to Princeton, leaving 600 men under Brig. Gen. Edward Mathew to guard the supplies. Lieutenant-General Cornwallis joined Grant at Princeton on the evening of the 1st, bringing with him additional troops. Cornwallis also brought with him an air of confidence and announced his intention to march directly against Washington at Trenton. He rejected a suggestion from Donop that a separate force move against Washington's right flank while the main force pinned his forces in Trenton.

The British advance, January 2, 1777

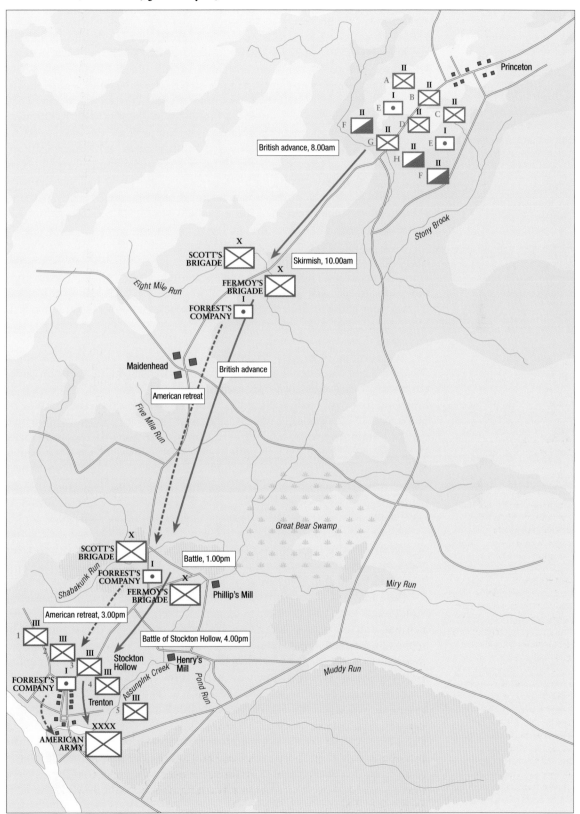

Princeton

II
A
I
E
B
F II
II
II C
G D II
H II
II E
F II

British advance, 8.00am

SCOTT'S X
BRIGADE

Skirmish, 10.00am

FERMOY'S X
BRIGADE
I
FORREST'S
COMPANY

Eight Mile Run

Stony Brook

Maidenhead

British advance

American retreat

Five Mile Run

Great Bear Swamp

Miry Run

SCOTT'S X
BRIGADE
I
FORREST'S
COMPANY
FERMOY'S X
BRIGADE

Battle, 1.00pm

Phillip's Mill

Shabakunk Run

American retreat, 3.00pm

III
1
III
III
I 3
III
FORREST'S
COMPANY
4
III
Trenton
5
III

Stockton
Hollow
Henry's
Mill

Battle of Stockton Hollow, 4.00pm

Assunpink Creek

Pond Run

Muddy Run

XXXX
AMERICAN
ARMY

67

In anticipation of the general advance of the main army early on January 1, British light infantry and *Jäger*, commanded by Lieutenant-Colonel Robert Abercromby, pushed south to the Little Shabakunk Creek where they found Hand's riflemen waiting. A fierce fight continued through the morning, with the light infantry and *Jäger* unable to secure the "pass" between the two banks and eventually being forced back from the creek. Hessian grenadiers came to their support and drove Hand's men back as the fighting died down.

On the evening of January 1 Washington's war council met again. They knew that Cornwallis was intent on marching to Trenton with 8,000 men. The group discussed three possible options: one was for the main army to retire to join Cadwalader at Crosswicks, another was to call him to Trenton, the last option was to remain at Trenton and order him to attack New Brunswick. After conferring with Dr. Benjamin Rush, who had just returned from Cadwalader, the decision was taken to order Cadwalader to Trenton. Having taken stock of the area south of the Assunpink Creek consensus was that the army should offer battle at Trenton.

Washington ordered his men to take up positions along a high ridge on the south bank of the Assunpink Creek. The ridge commanded the approach from Trenton, which was restricted to a single stone bridge. Washington moved his headquarters to Jonathan Richmond's Tavern south of the creek. Cadwalader and Mifflin, arrived from Crosswicks at daybreak on January 2.

Battle of Assunpink Creek

On the morning of January 2 Cornwallis commanded 9,500 men, including 60 cavalry and 28 pieces of artillery. Cornwallis detached Grant's 4th Brigade, temporarily commanded by Lieutenant-Colonel Mawhood, to remain in Princeton as a rearguard, with orders to march to Trenton on the morning of January 3, 1776. In addition to the 17th, 40th and 55th foot Mawhood also had one mounted troop and three dismounted troops of the 16th Light Dragoons, three 2-gun artillery sections, supply wagons and several companies of men from various regiments that had been on detached duty in New York. These men were also to march with him to Trenton to rejoin their parent regiments. Brigadier-General Leslie's 2nd Brigade was left at Maidenhead as Cornwallis advanced toward Trenton with approximately 8,000 men.

The British advance on January 2 was led by Donop. Two companies of *Jäger*, one mounted one on foot, supported by a company of Hessian grenadiers and two troops of the 16th Light Dragoons were in the van, followed by British light infantry, artillery and British and Hessian grenadiers. As this advance force moved through the British positions north of Maidenhead American riflemen engaged them. At 10.00am a series of running battles began as the Americans attempted to delay the British approach. Several times Hand's men, supported by Haussegger, Scott and the artillery, took the British under fire, forcing the lead elements to deploy for battle only to find the Americans had retired. At about 1.00pm American resistance stiffened at Shabakunk Creek, three miles from Trenton. While his men were engaging the enemy at Shabakunk Creek, Brig. Gen. Fermoy, without explanation, wheeled his horse and rode back to Trenton, leaving Col. Hand in command. Although the creek was fordable in several places the Americans removed the wooden bridge and occupied dense woods on the south bank. The Hessians and British approached the creek over open fields. After trading volleys with Hand's men the British brought up their artillery. As the British were peppering the American positions with cannon fire

The Douglass House served as headquarters for Brig. Gen. St. Clair and was used by Washington to hold a war council on the evening of January 2, 1777, at which it was agreed that the army should retire from Trenton, move around the British left flank and attack the British positions at Princeton. (Author's collection)

Washington, along with Knox and Greene, rode up to take stock of the situation. Washington explained to Hand the importance of delaying the British march and "gave orders for as obstinate a stand as could be made on that ground, without hazarding the [artillery] pieces ..."

By 3.30pm the entire weight of the British and Hessian forces compelled Hand to order a retirement. Scott's 5th Virginia Regiment, supported by Colonel Mordecai Buckner's 6th Virginia Regiment retreated southwest toward Assunpink Creek, keeping Minnigerode's composite grenadier battalion and the remnants of Rall's Brigade from flanking Hand's riflemen and the German battalion, which retired along the main road to several hastily constructed small redoubts at Stockton Hollow. On a small rise overlooking a ravine Captain Forrest's two guns, supported by Hand with over 500 infantry, confronted the British as they advanced. Daylight was already fading as Cornwallis was again forced to deploy his guns to engage the Americans. Scott and Buckner were unable to stop the British flanking movement and Hand ordered the artillery withdrawn and slowly retreated with his infantry through Trenton.

Washington ordered Hitchcock's Brigade to cover the retreat of Hand's men, now exhausted after a day of fighting. Hitchcock's Brigade advanced up Queen Street to Fourth Street, where Hand's men and guns passed though them and retired to the bridge. Seeing Hand's Brigade retire through Hitchcock's regiments toward the bridge, the British sought to cut off their retreat by leaving the road and marching directly toward the bridge. American artillery, posted on the higher ground beyond Assunpink Creek, fired into the heads and flanks of the enemy columns, delaying their advance. The Grenadier Regiments von Linsingen and von Block grenadier regiments along with the *Jäger* deployed to Hitchcock's front while British light infantry moved down King Street toward the bridge, firing into Hitchcock's flank from between houses. An officer from the Fusilier Regiment von Knyphausen noted "the rebel generals did their utmost and withdrew in fairly good order through Trentown, occupied the bridge and took up their positions on the far side of the entrenchments, which they had thrown up during our absence."

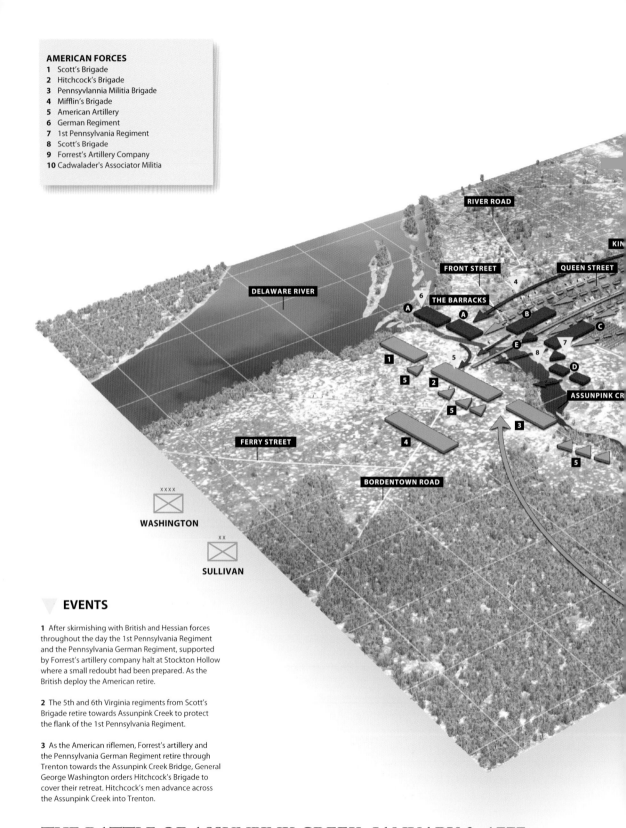

AMERICAN FORCES
1 Scott's Brigade
2 Hitchcock's Brigade
3 Pennsyvlannia Militia Brigade
4 Mifflin's Brigade
5 American Artillery
6 German Regiment
7 1st Pennsylvania Regiment
8 Scott's Brigade
9 Forrest's Artillery Company
10 Cadwalader's Associator Militia

RIVER ROAD

FRONT STREET

QUEEN STREET

KIN

DELAWARE RIVER

THE BARRACKS

ASSUNPINK CR

FERRY STREET

BORDENTOWN ROAD

xxxx
WASHINGTON

xx
SULLIVAN

▼ EVENTS

1 After skirmishing with British and Hessian forces throughout the day the 1st Pennsylvania Regiment and the Pennsylvania German Regiment, supported by Forrest's artillery company halt at Stockton Hollow where a small redoubt had been prepared. As the British deploy the American retire.

2 The 5th and 6th Virginia regiments from Scott's Brigade retire towards Assunpink Creek to protect the flank of the 1st Pennsylvania Regiment.

3 As the American riflemen, Forrest's artillery and the Pennsylvania German Regiment retire through Trenton towards the Assunpink Creek Bridge, General George Washington orders Hitchcock's Brigade to cover their retreat. Hitchcock's men advance across the Assunpink Creek into Trenton.

THE BATTLE OF ASSUNPINK CREEK, JANUARY 2, 1777
The British under Cornwallis fail to force Assunpink Creek in the face of a strong American defense

PENNINGTON ROAD

BRITISH FORCES
A British light infantry battalions
B Grenadier battalions von Linsingen and von Block
C British infantry
D Hessian *Jäger* companies
E Hessian artillery units

X X

CORNWALLIS

BEAKES ESTATE

1

6

9

7

A

A

PRINCETON ROAD

B

C

8

D

2

D

REET

-Z

6 After failing to push across the creek British light infantry, joined by Hessian *Jäger* occupy houses near the creek.

7 General Cornwallis orders Hessian artillery to deploy to support the attacks of the Hessian and British grenadiers.

8 The Hessian Grenadier battalions von Linsingen and von Block attempt to cross the Assunpink Creek bridge in column but are driven back, leaving dead and wounded littering the bridge. Cornwallis orders British infantry to twice attempt to push across but intense American artillery and musket fire stalls both attacks.

4 British light infantry move around the American left flank and try to cut off the American line of retreat to the Assunpink Creek.

5 The 1st Pennsylvania Regiment and Forrest's artillery cross the Assunpink without incident but the Pennsylvania German Regiment becomes disorganized as Hitchcock's Brigade falls back and attempts to retire across the bridge. American artillery fires over their heads into the pursuing British and Hessian infantry. British light infantry attempt to ford the creek but are driven back by American musket fire.

9 Concerned about the continued British attacks on the Assunpink Bridge, Washington orders Colonel Cadwalader's Philadelphia Associator Militia to move to reinforce the American defenses.

Note: Gridlines are shown at intervals of 250 yards/288m

Although the British pursuit was slowed by the artillery the bridge became a choke point as Hand's men and artillery pushed onto the narrow structure and Hitchcock's Brigade was pushed slowly back. Washington, seeing that the slightest indiscipline would lead to disaster placed himself at the southern end of the bridge, where the retreating soldiers could see him and rally to his steady leadership. Hitchcock's men added to the confusion at the bridge. With the Hessian grenadiers bearing down on them and British light infantry threatening their flank discipline began to breakdown and they joined the refugees at the bridge. In the ensuing confusion the Pennsylvania German Regiment appears to have suffered severe casualties, including the capture of Col. Nicholas Haussegger.

By firing over the heads of the crowd at the bridge, up King and Queen streets, the American artillery was able to forestall the Hessian attack on Hitchcock's men. Washington directed Hitchcock to bring his men across the creek and deploy in a nearby field, between the Delaware River and the bridge, protected by Knox's artillery arrayed along the ridge. Scott's Virginia Brigade was given the task of defending the bridge, supported by 18 guns.

Washington occupied a strong position, nearly three miles long along the south side of the Assunpink from the Delaware River to Phillips Ford. Although the failing light limited the effectiveness of musketry, the rising ground allowed him to deploy his artillery. At several places the Americans had constructed hasty breastworks. Of the two upper fords Phillips Mill was easily fordable and Washington deployed several artillery batteries and St. Clair's Brigade to prevent a British crossing. The Assunpink at Henry's Mill was deeper and the water so swift that the British infantry would find it impossible to cross.

Militia units were integrated between the Continental brigades. Ewing's Pennsylvania Militia and Newcomb's New Jersey Militia were placed around the bridge, while Cadwalader's men were deployed with artillery on Washington's right, one mile from the bridge. Mercer's Brigade was posted a mile beyond Cadwalader's.

With little daylight left to assist their attack Cornwallis and Donop drew up their forces on the high ground north of the creek. The sight of the British and Hessian troops deploying for battle caused many on the American side to despair. Washington and his lieutenants knew they were in a precarious position. They could not cross the enemy's front to move to Princeton, and retreat into southern New Jersey would provide little relief. Even if they wanted to re-cross the Delaware there were neither enough boats nor time. Once again the future of the Revolution hung in the balance.

Corwallis first tried to find a weak spot in the American line. British light infantry and Hessian *Jäger* moved to occupy the houses across from Hitchcock's Brigade deployed between the bridge and the Delaware River. After trading shots with the Americans the light infantry and *Jäger* pushed down to the edge of the Assunpink where they attracted a storm of fire from American infantry and artillery, forcing them back to the protection of the buildings.

Cornwallis next tried to use the Hessian grenadiers to bludgeon his way over the Assunpink Bridge. *Jäger* kept up a steady fire from the houses along the creek and artillery was deployed to support the attack. Colonel Charles Scott, commanding the Virginia infantry defending the bridge, addressed his men, "you know the old Boss has put us here to defend this bridge; and by God it must be done, let what will come."

A column of Hessian grenadiers pushed forward to the narrow bridge and was met with fire from Scott's men and the supporting artillery. Before they reached the middle of the bridge American fire had shredded the column killing or wounding 31 and forcing 29 to surrender.

With the repulse of the Hessians, Cornwallis ordered his British infantry to try and gain a foothold. Their first attempt ended with the British column stalling at the head of the bridge, leaving dead and wounded littering the ground. The British infantry regrouped and surged ahead again, this time forcing their way onto the bridge before they too were forced back. The American infantry raised a shout as the British retired. Cornwallis tried one last time, sending another strong column to capture the bridge. The American artillery pounded the British infantry and Washington ordered Cadwalader's men to reinforce Scott at the bridge. The British again broke against the bridge and retreated into the darkness, ending the battle of Assunpink Creek. American casualties were estimated at about 50, while the British and Hessian losses exceeded 350. British casualties for the entire day of fighting were estimated at 500.

Cornwallis withdrew his bloodied units out of Trenton to the woods on the south bank of the Shabakunk Creek, leaving a couple of light infantry battalions to watch the Americans. He had already decided that he would turn Washington's right flank by assaulting St. Clair's Brigade at Phillips Mill at first light. Cornwallis's staff was divided on the course of action. Some, like Grant, agreed that the men, exhausted after a daylong pursuit and a brief but brutal twilight battle, should be allowed to rest. To their minds Washington had nowhere to go. Others, including Sir William Erskine, quartermaster general, noted unusual rebel activity and urged Cornwallis to take immediate action. Erskine told Cornwallis that "if Washington is the general I take him to be, the army will not be found in the morning." Cornwallis reassured Erskine that "we've got the old fox safe now. We'll go over and bag him in the morning." Still, concerned about the strength of the American artillery, Cornwallis sent for the Princeton garrison to reinforce his force.

Advance to Princeton

On the American side the men built large bonfires to warm themselves as the temperature dropped. Some tried to find food while others found a place to rest on the cold ground. At St. Clair's headquarters at the Alexander Douglass House Washington held yet another council of war. This time there was very little debate; they all understood the seriousness of their situation. It is unclear who proposed the course of action to be taken. Washington certainly was aware of the vulnerability of his position. Joseph Reed, who grew up in Trenton and attended Princeton, reminded Washington that he and a troop of the Philadelphia Light Horse had ridden through the area east of Trenton over the last few days and found no enemy. Washington also had the spy map provided by Cadwalader which showed the back roads that could be used to reach Princeton. Among the militia there were several local farmers who agreed to act as guides. At the same time Washington also recognized the risk of marching across the front of the enemy. If Cornwallis discovered the movement and pushed across the creek he could have shattered the Americans and defeated them in detail.

The weather over the preceding days had been warm with rain, turning the roads into muddy tracks and limiting the ability to move artillery. Providentially the weather once again changed. Temperatures dropped throughout the evening, freezing the muddy ground and allowing the artillery and baggage to be moved. The baggage and heavy artillery were sent off to

BATTLE OF ASSUNPINK CREEK, JANUARY 2, 1777 (pp. 74–75)

On January 2, 1777, Brigadier-General Fermoy's Brigade and Colonel Scott's Brigade, reinforced by Captain Forrest's artillery company, was deployed east of Trenton. The remainder of the American Army was positioned on the rising ground south of the Assunpink Creek. The British, commanded by Lieutenant-General Cornwallis with 8,000 men, advanced from Maidenhead early that morning. Throughout the day Fermoy's and Scott's troops fought a series of skirmishes with the British and Hessian advance guard, delaying their advance. Late in the day Hitchcock's Brigade was ordered across the Assunpink Creek to support the Americans, as they fell back into Trenton. Fermoy's men passed through Hitchcock's Brigade and both groups made their way in some haste to the bridge with British light infantry and Hessian *Jäger* in close pursuit. In the fading twilight panic began to take hold of the American's as they retired across the bridge in some confusion. British troops occupied buildings near the creek and began to probe the American defenses.

Washington, observing the retirement from the southern bank of the bridge, helped restore order and directed

Hitchcock's Brigade to deploy west of the bridge to counter the advance of the light infantry and *Jäger*. The illustration depicts American officers deploying Hitchcock's men to take up positions at the creek. Hitchcock's Brigade was composed of New England regiments, which were generally uniformed in brown coats with red facings, (**1**) while some officers retained blue coats (**2**). In the distance can be seen the bridge over Assunpink Creek (**3**) and Stacy's Mill (**4**). British light infantry can also be seen advancing onto the bridge from the north bank. (**5**)

Hitchcock's Brigade joined in repulsing several assaults by British and Hessian grenadiers to force their way across the Assunpink Bridge. These attacks were driven back by concentrated musket and artillery fire and Cornwallis called off the action, believing he could destroy Washington's Army the next day. During the night the Americans retired, sending their baggage and the bulk of their artillery toward Philadelphia while Washington marched towards Princeton with the remainder of the army.

Burlington under Brig. Gen. Stephen, while a strong rearguard of New Jersey Militia continued to maintain the fires and go through the motions of improving the entrenchments. The wheels of the remaining cannon were wrapped in old cloth to muffle the noise and the army marched to the east toward their first objective, Princeton, which lay 12 miles away, and then beyond to New Brunswick. Some units began moving around 10.00pm under strict silence and only senior officers were told of the intended destination. The bulk of the army was under way by midnight.

Despite the best efforts of the Americans who remained to screen the army's movement, Cornwallis began to receive reports of unusual activity on the American side and clear indications that the American Army was on the move. With the surprise attack on Trenton fresh in his mind Cornwallis feared Washington was planning a similar attack on his men. In response he directed the Guards and British and Hessian grenadiers to protect the crossings of Henry's Mill and Phillips Mill.

The movement of large numbers of cold and exhausted soldiers, over unfamiliar roads, in the dark of night, inevitably resulted in confusion. At one point a unit of militia panicked at the sight of an unfamiliar neighboring unit, spreading alarm and creating panic in other units, who joined them in flight to Bordentown and Burlington. After marching a half-mile to the southeast the army moved east, across the Pond Run. The route was a narrow country road recently cut through a wooded area, littered with stumps and roots that bedeviled the Americans. With Brig. Gen. Mercer's Brigade, totaling roughly 325 men, leading the column from Pond Run the Americans crossed several more small creeks, skirted the Great Bear Swamp and crossed the upper reaches of the Assunpink Creek at Rozel's Mill. Washington's men were making for the Quaker Bridge Road.

The Quaker Bridge Road connected the village of Crosswicks with the Friends Meeting House. The Quaker Road was a traveled rather than a crude path and the Americans made good time. Mercer's men reached the Quaker Bridge as daylight was breaking, about 6.50am. To their frustration they found the bridge unable to support the weight of the artillery and ammunition carts. Work began immediately on construction of a second makeshift bridge to allow the artillery to cross. Washington used this delay to allow the trailing units to catch up and the men to rest. He also decided to split his force in a manner similar to the advance toward Trenton. Major-General Greene was given command of the left wing while Maj. Gen. Sullivan was assigned the bulk of the army. At 7.20am, as the sun began to rise over the horizon, the army set out again to march the six miles to Princeton.

The battle of Princeton

Mercer's Brigade led Greene's Division along the Stony Brook toward Worth's Mill and the bridge over the main post road between Princeton and Trenton. Mercer's Brigade was composed of remnants of Continental and rifle regiments from Virginia, Maryland and Delaware, supported by Captain Daniel Neil's two-gun company. Cadwalader's Philadelphia Associators, totaling approximately 1,150 men, including the Marine company and Captain Joseph Moulder's two-gun company followed Mercer. Although the road ran parallel to the creek the ground on both sides rose quickly, screening Mercer's men from view. Greene's men had two objectives. First, a small force would be posted at the bridge to delay the expected advance of Cornwallis' force from Trenton. The remainder of the command was expected to advance

ABOVE LEFT

Council of War by William E. Pedrick. Washington and his staff are shown discussing their options at the Douglass House. Washington used these councils to explore fully potential strategies. Although there is no conclusive evidence who first suggested the move to Princeton, Washington had information from Brig. Gen. Cadwalader about the disposition of British defenses at Princeton and a recent report from Col. Joseph Reed, who had ridden with a small unit of the Philadelphia Light Horse toward Princeton several days before. (Courtesy of the Old Barracks Association, Trenton, NJ)

ABOVE RIGHT

The Quaker Meeting House was a well-known location in the Princeton area, located near the Saw Mill Road used by Sullivan's column as they advanced toward Princeton. (Author's collection)

by the post road into Princeton, blocking any potential breakout of the garrison toward Cornwallis and focusing the defenders' attention to the west as the rest of the army attacked from the south and east.

Sullivan's Division, totaling over 5,000 men, was led by St. Clair's New England Brigade, followed by Mifflin's Pennsylvania Brigade and accompanied by various militia units. As they crossed the Quaker Bridge, Sullivan's men turned east to march along higher ground, following the Saw Mill Road that would take them into Princeton. Sullivan and his staff rode with the vanguard. As they looked back toward Worth's Mill they were shocked to see a column of red-uniformed men. Two British cavalry quickly rode to the top of a small hill and then disappeared toward the column.

The horsemen from the 16th Light Dragoons reported the unimaginable to Lt. Col. Charles Mawhood. American infantry was marching toward Princeton. Mawhood, commanding the 4th Brigade, composed of the 17th, 40th and 55th foot, reacted quickly. The Americans had found him marching with the 17th and 55th foot and an assortment of replacement companies for the 42nd Foot, British grenadiers and light infantry, mounted and dismounted light dragoons, artillery and supply wagons in response to an urgent request from Cornwallis in Trenton. Mawhood's column, totaling 700 men, had set out just before sunrise and the head of the column had just marched up the hill beyond Stony Creek when they discovered the Americans. Although the 17th Foot and the light dragoons had crossed Stony Brook the remainder of Mawhood's men were strung out along the Princeton–Trenton Road.

Mawhood briefly considered his options before ordering his vanguard, the 17th Foot, to recross the Stony Brook bridge to confront the Americans. He directed the 55th Foot, which was still some distance from the bridge to accompany the wagons back to Princeton and assist the 40th Foot in defending the town.

While Mawhood's column was reversing course to confront Sullivan's force, the British were unaware of the location of Mercer's and Cadwalader's men marching along the sunken road. At the same time, although Mercer had seen the mounted scouts he could not see the main British column. Washington, who could see both Mawhood's men and Mercer's column, dispatched a courier to Greene alerting him to the danger and directing him to attack the enemy. It is doubtful that Washington was aware of the full strength of the British force. Mercer immediately detached a force of riflemen

The American advance to Princeton

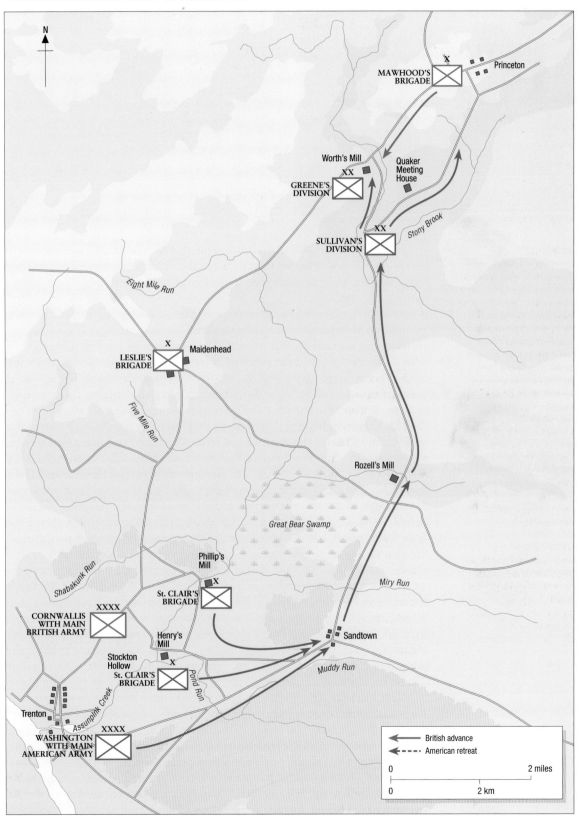

N

MAWHOOD'S
BRIGADE
X

Princeton

Worth's Mill

Quaker
Meeting
House

GREENE'S
DIVISION
XX

Stony Brook

SULLIVAN'S
DIVISION
XX

Eight Mile Run

LESLIE'S
BRIGADE
X
Maidenhead

Five Mile Run

Rozell's Mill

Great Bear Swamp

Miry Run

Phillip's
Mill

St. CLAIR'S
BRIGADE
X

Shabakunk Run

CORNWALLIS
WITH MAIN
BRITISH ARMY
XXXX

Henry's
Mill

Sandtown

Muddy Run

Stockton
Hollow
X

St. CLAIR'S
BRIGADE

Pond Run

Trenton

Assunpink Creek

WASHINGTON
WITH MAIN
AMERICAN ARMY
XXXX

British advance

American retreat

0   2 miles

0   2 km

ABOVE LEFT
Cemetery at Quaker Meeting House. At least one casualty from the battle of Princeton is believed to be buried in the cemetery. Some accounts of the Princeton battle suggest that Cadwalader's militia retired as far as the Quaker Meeting House as they attempted to rally. (Author's collection)

ABOVE RIGHT
Mercer's column marched along a road adjacent to the Stony Brook unseen by Mawhood's column moving from Princeton to Trenton. Both the road and Mercer's column were sheltered from view by the British. Mercer's men climbed the steep bank on the right and surprised the British as they advanced toward the William Clarke Farm. (Author's collection)

and a small unit of Continentals, totaling approximately 120 men, to climb the slope on his right, while the remainder of his infantry and artillery followed. The steep slope limited the unhindered movement of formed units, particularly artillery.

Mawhood, mounted on a brown pony and accompanied by two spaniels, led his men along the road and then turned south climbing a slope from the post road to higher ground. Mounted light dragoons rode in advance and were surprised by the appearance of Mercer's vanguard suddenly appearing on their right flank. Mawhood reacted to this new development by deploying his two cannon, forming the 17th Foot in line and ordering them to shed their packs. He also directed the dismounted light dragoons to occupy the William Clarke Farm and the adjacent orchard.

Mercer, riding at the head of his men, also noted that the Clarke Farm would provide a good defensive position and ordered his men toward the orchard and buildings. The light dragoons lined up behind the northern fence line as Mercer and his men pushed through a narrow gate and advanced through the orchard. As they made their way through the trees the light dragoons rose up and fired a volley that clipped the branches above the Americans' heads but did little damage. Mercer's men returned fire, driving the light dragoons to take cover behind the northern fence line. The rest of Mercer's command, approximately 200 men, entered the orchard to support the riflemen as Mawhood marched forward with 450 men. At 40 yards Captain John Fleming of the 1st Virginia Regiment shouted in a steady voice, "Gentlemen, dress before you make ready." From the British line a voice replied, "Damn you, we will dress you" as the line erupted in flames, but this volley also went high. Two more volleys from the Americans riddled the British line, killing and wounding officers and men. The British steadied themselves and fired again, this time finding their marks. As the Americans recoiled Mawhood ordered a bayonet charge. Without bayonets the Americans were defenseless. Mercer ordered the retreat as his horse went down. A British soldier knocked him down with a musket butt. Surrounded and called on to surrender, Mercer refused. As he struck out with his sword he was bayoneted several times and left for dead.

Haslett, who had accompanied Mercer, now took command and briefly tried to rally the men before being killed. On the left of the American line Captain Neil died at his guns, deployed in an open field next to the orchard, as the British overwhelmed the American line, driving the survivors back through the orchard and buildings of the William Clarke Farm. Cadwalader's militia, entering the battlefield in march column, found the survivors of Mercer's Brigade streaming out of the farmstead toward the Thomas Clarke Farm, situated on higher ground. In order to attack the British, Cadwalader's three battalions needed to deploy into line under fire, a complicated maneuver even for veteran troops. The lead elements of Cadwalader's column began deploying as the first scattered groups of Mercer's panicked men made their way up the hill. These men careened into the Associators, further disorganizing them. In their growing confusion the Associators began to fire ragged volleys toward the British, who were well beyond the effective range of the American muskets.

The remainder of Cadwalader's men inclined toward the Thomas Clarke Farm. Moulder's two-gun 4-pdr company moved to the right of the Thomas Clarke Farmhouse and deployed. Some of Mercer's men, reassured by the appearance of Cadwalader's militia, rallied on the far side of the Thomas Clarke Farm and returned, taking position among haystacks and outbuildings on either side of Moulder's guns.

The British, having driven Mercer's men from the William Clarke Farm, re-formed their lines and advanced their artillery toward the Americans gathered at the Thomas Clarke Farm. The British light infantry and dismounted 16th Light Dragoons supported the 17th Foot. British artillerymen also wheeled one of the captured guns into position to support their assault. As they moved forward Mawhood's men saw Cadwalader's column streaming up the slope to the Thomas Clarke Farm. The 17th Foot and its supporting units stopped at a fence line in the valley between the two farms. As they moved toward the enemy Cadwalader tried to steady his men. The Associators were still suffering from the impact of Mercer's survivors and moved tentatively toward the British line.

LEFT
Sullivan's column, marching along the Saw Mill Road, encountered small patches of woods like these, which masked their advance from the British. These wooded areas also provided some protection for Cadwalader's militia to rally after their initial repulse around the Thomas Clarke Farm. (Author's collection)

RIGHT
Modern roadway, west of Stony Brook Bridge, showing the steep slope that a portion of Mawhood's column climbed before they observed Sullivan's men marching toward Princeton. It was from this approximate location that Washington sighted Mawhood's column. (Author's collection)

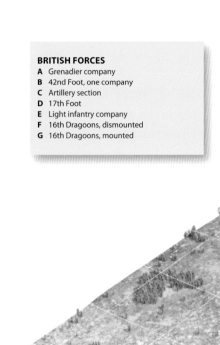

BRITISH FORCES
- **A** Grenadier company
- **B** 42nd Foot, one company
- **C** Artillery section
- **D** 17th Foot
- **E** Light infantry company
- **F** 16th Dragoons, dismounted
- **G** 16th Dragoons, mounted

WORTH'S MILL

STONY BROOK CREEK

THOMAS CLARKE FARM

QUAKER ROAD

SAW MILL ROAD

WASHINGTON

SULLIVAN

▼ EVENTS

1 Washington, hearing the firing between Mercer and Mawhood's men, rides back toward the Thomas Clarke Farm. He joins Col. Cadwalader, who is trying to rally his Philadelphia Associator Militia. Washington and Cadwalader direct the militia to retire behind the Thomas Clarke Farm, where they are reorganized and rallied.

2 As the militia are being rallied Moulder's Company of artillery, supported by elements of Mercer's Brigade and Cadwalader's militia, hold off the advance of the British infantry. The mounted troop of the 16th Light Dragoons attempts to outflank the American right. Moulder's artillery drive the British cavalry off with several volley's of grapeshot.

3 As Washington and Cadwalader order the militia and remnants of Mercer's Brigade forward, riflemen and militia light infantry extend the American line to the left, moving around the flank of the British line.

4 Having rallied Cadwalader's Associator Militia Washington leads two battalions forward past the Thomas Clarke Farmhouse and down a gentle slope towards the British line.

5 Cadwalader, taking command of the third Associator militia battalion, moves to the right of the Thomas Clarke Farm, into an adjoining field. Cadwalader's men march toward the British artillery, supported by the 42nd Foot and a grenadier company, deployed on a small rise just south of the William Clarke Farm.

6 Hitchcock's Brigade, accompanied by the 1st Pennsylvania Regiment and a single artillery section also advance towards the British artillery.

7 Hand's men join with Hitchcock's Brigade and Cadwalader's militia and engage in a lively exchange of musket fire with the British infantry.

8 As Washington and his men advance towards the British line, American light infantry and riflemen begin to filter around the British flank. After several volleys the 17th Foot, along with the light infantry and dismounted dragoons begin to disintegrate and small groups fight their way through the American militia and riflemen to retreat.

9 Hitchcock and Hand's men overwhelm the 42nd Foot and grenadiers, pushing them back and capturing the British artillery. The surviving British infantry retreats towards Princeton.

10 Washington leads his men in a short pursuit of the retreating British forces, stopping at the Thomas Olden House. While small groups of riflemen continue to pursue the retreating British Washington orders an artillery company and small force of milita to defend the Stony Brook Bridge. He rejoins Sullivan's column which resumes its advance towards Princeton.

11 Lieutenant-Colonel Mawhood, with a group of 17th Foot, light infantry and dismounted grenadiers breaks through the American militia and retreats towards Princeton.

THE BATTLE OF PRINCETON, JANUARY 3, 1777
Washington's men destroy the British 4th Brigade

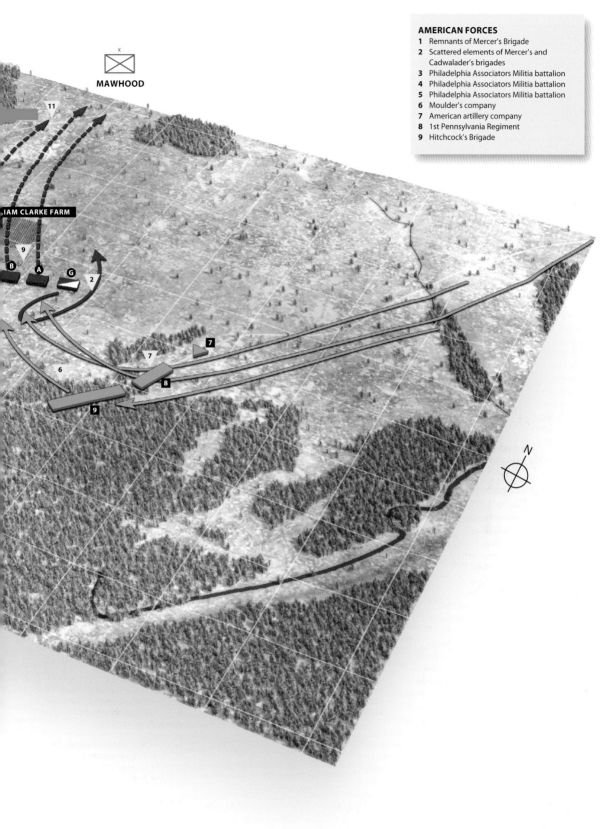

MAWHOOD

WILLIAM CLARKE FARM

AMERICAN FORCES

1 Remnants of Mercer's Brigade
2 Scattered elements of Mercer's and Cadwalader's brigades
3 Philadelphia Associators Militia battalion
4 Philadelphia Associators Militia battalion
5 Philadelphia Associators Militia battalion
6 Moulder's company
7 American artillery company
8 1st Pennsylvania Regiment
9 Hitchcock's Brigade

Note: Gridlines are shown at intervals of 250 yards/288m

The British responded with a series of telling volleys that threw Cadwalader's men into confusion, causing them to recoil 40 yards back toward the Clarke Farm. As Cadwalader's militia retired General Washington rode over the ridge and into the milling confusion. Washington had been riding at the head of Sullivan's column moving toward Princeton when the first musket shots, followed by the low report of cannon fire, echoed over the fields. Washington immediately rode back toward the firing, accompanied by the mounted Associator troop and Hand's riflemen. Hitchcock's Brigade, under the command of Major Israel Angell, marching in the rear of Sullivan's column was ordered to follow Washington. As he came upon Cadwalader's confused men he quickly sized up the situation and realized the militia could be not be rallied under fire. He ordered Cadwalader to fall back beyond the Clarke Farm to a wooded area behind a small ridge to re-form. Moulder's company stood firm as Cadwalader retired, engaging in a duel with the British cannon near the William Clarke Farm. A few militia, including Rodney's Delaware Light Infantry, remained with Moulder, taking cover in haystacks on their right.

Moulder's guns kept the 17th Foot, which remained stationary in the valley, at bay, while the British guns on the opposite hill raked the militia scattered around the house and haystacks. Rodney's men noted a small mounted group of 16th Light Dragoons moving tentatively on their right. Moulder drove them away with a round of grapeshot.

As Moulder and the scattered militia held off the British, Washington rallied the main body of Mercer's and Cadwalader's men. Washington appealed to the militia, shouting, "parade with us, my brave fellows. There is but a handful of the enemy and we will have them directly." Slowly the men fell into line, forming two units. Washington led one group directly back over the hill, past the Clarke Farm and down toward the 17th Foot. As the militia marched toward the 17th Foot, elements of the militia light infantry moved off to the left. As his aides watched in horror, Washington led from the front into a storm of musket fire but emerged unscathed.

Cadwalader led the other group of Associators to the right of the Thomas Clarke Farm toward the British artillery deployed south of the William Clarke Farm. At the same time, Hitchcock's New England Brigade, totaling approximately 350 men, preceded by Hand's 200 riflemen, began to deploy to the right of Moulder's position. Trailing behind was a New England artillery company that took up position on the far right of the American line.

View from the Quaker Meeting House toward Saw Mill Road. Thomas and William Clarke's grandfather owned the farm visible in the trees, while their father owned the farm visible immediately to the right. There is still uncertainty over the exact location of the Saw Mill Road. (Author's collection)

Hitchcock's men had to stop briefly to allow Cadwalader's column to pass to their front as they deployed into line. Both groups began a steady march toward the British artillery, which was supported by the grenadier companies and elements of the 42nd Foot.

With Hitchcock and Hand's appearance on the field the 17th Foot was in danger of being outflanked on their left. On their right the militia light infantry companies were also moving around their other flank threatening to envelop them. The supporting British companies from the grenadiers and 42nd Foot moved forward from their positions south of the William Clarke farm to protect the 17th Foot's left flank, while the 17th Foot moved to their right to close the gap. The Associators, Hand's riflemen and Hitchcock's Continentals poured fire into the British line.

The American pressure finally cracked the British regulars, fracturing the 17th Foot into small, disorganized groups. One large group lowered their bayonets and drove through Cadwalader's militia toward the Stony Brook Bridge. The remaining dismounted light dragoons joined them. After making a momentary stand at the bridge the two groups retired in disorder over the Stony Brook and up the hill toward Maidenhead and safety. The Americans swarmed over the British guns, cutting down the crews. Washington, elated at his success, shouted, "It's a fine fox chase, my boys!" Together with his men he halted at Thomas Olden's House. American riflemen pursued small groups of British survivors across the countryside. Washington ordered Colonel James Porter's Philadelphia Militia with Captain Forrest's artillery to pull down the Stony Brook Bridge and defend the crossing against Cornwallis's inevitable advance.

During the 45-minute struggle at the Clarke farms the British 55th Foot stood idle in a small wood on higher ground, later known as Mercer Hill, several hundred yards to the east. The 55th Foot had been ordered there by Mawhood along with four pieces of artillery. While the 17th Foot fought at the Clarke farms the 55th Foot watched Sullivan's column stopped along the Saw Mill Road. As the bulk of his force retired in disorder to the west, Mawhood and a small group retreated east. Along the way Mawhood ordered Major Cornelius Cuyler, commander of the 55th Foot, to retire to Princeton to aid in its defense. While the artillery returned to Princeton the 55th Foot took up position along a ridge behind Frog Hollow, a small brook flowing through a deep ravine southwest of town. Behind this position was a small redoubt.

ABOVE LEFT
The existing stone bridge over Stony Brook. At the time of the battle of Princeton a wooden bridge stood at this approximate location. Mawhood's column was in the process of crossing the bridge when George Washington observed them. At same time the British observed Maj. Gen. Sullivan's column and Mawhood ordered the British column to retire toward Princeton. (Author's collection)

ABOVE RIGHT
The battle of Princeton took place near the Thomas Clarke Farm. The original section of the house is shown on the right. The section of the home on the left was added after the battle. The Thomas Clarke House is now used as the Princeton Battlefield museum. (Author's collection)

BATTLE OF PRINCETON (pp. 86–87)

After slipping away from the main British Army late on the night of January 2–3, the American Army advanced toward the British garrison at Princeton. The British 4th Brigade, commanded by Lt. Col. Mawhood, marched early on the morning of January 3 toward Trenton to reinforce Cornwallis' main force. As the British began to cross Stony Creek at Worth's Mill and climb the hill on the west bank they observed Sullivan's Division moving along the Saw Mill Road, east of the Thomas Clarke Farm. Unseen to the British, Mercer's and Cadwalader's brigades marched on a sunken road along Stony Creek towards the bridge.

Mawhood directed the 40th Foot and the baggage train to return to Princeton while he led a mixed force, which included the 17th Foot, artillery, a company of grenadiers, light infantry and 42nd Foot, along with troops of dismounted and mounted 16th Light Dragoons to engage the Americans. The British attacked and routed Mercer's men, who had occupied the William Clarke Farm, fatally wounding Mercer. Cadwalader's Brigade of Philadelphia Associator Militia, marching to support Mercer, were thrown into confusion by Mercer's fleeing men and both groups retreated to an area south of the Thomas Clarke Farm. General George Washington, watching the shattering of Mercer's command, directed Colonel Hand's

riflemen and Hitchcock's Brigade to attack Mawhood's force. Washington rode to the Thomas Clarke Farm and assisted Cadwalader in rallying the militia and the remnants of Mercer's command. Mawhood, with the 17th Foot, dismounted 16th Light Dragoons and light infantry moved towards the Thomas Clarke Farm, stopping at a fenceline. Captain Moulder's artillery company, deployed near the Thomas Clarke Farm, and supported by elements of Mercer's men, engaged British artillery near the William Clarke Farm.

Washington and Cadwalader led the re-formed American militia and Continentals past the Thomas Clarke Farm and down a slight slope towards Mawhood, The larger American force outflanked Mawhood's line, wrapping around and threatening to cut off their line of retreat. After trading several volleys the British line began to disintegrate.

The scene shows a mixed force of British 17th Foot (**1**), light infantry (**2**) and dismounted dragoons (**3**) breaking out of the tightening circle of Americans, which includes Philadelphia Associators (**4**), militia light infantry (**5**) and a small group of Marines (**6**). Similar groups, including one led by Lt. Col. Mawhood, fought their way through the Americans and retreated.

Sullivan and his men also remained stationary along the Saw Mill Road while the battle raged. With Mawhood driven from the field Sullivan resumed his advance. Major Cuyler's position at Frog Hollow covered the Saw Mill Road approach. He detached a platoon of the 55th Foot to attempt to ambush Sullivan's column as it approached. Sullivan responded by deploying several regiments, pushed back the detachment and then advanced against the 55th Foot. Parties of American troops threatened both flanks of the 55th Foot causing it to retire to the redoubt. Sullivan followed and deployed two cannon. Once again the British position was made untenable as American units threatened to envelop the redoubt and the 55th Foot retired to another redoubt near the Princeton campus with Sullivan hard on their heels. The new position proved no more secure for the 55th Foot and the regiment surrendered to Sullivan.

A small number of survivors from the 17th and 55th foot took refuge in Nassau Hall and prepared to defend the building. Captain Alexander Hamilton brought up his two-gun company and after several rounds these men also surrendered. The British delaying actions beginning at Frog Hollow bought Mawhood precious time to evacuate the bulk of his supplies and artillery. Although the British were able to retire, the ensuing pursuit by the Americans threw them into a panic. Several artillery pieces were abandoned and the 40th Foot lost over 90 men missing or captured.

British casualties were heavy. Mawhood's command suffered 232 killed or wounded. American casualties were not recorded, but it is likely that Washington had approximately 40 killed and perhaps twice that number wounded. Brigadier-General Mercer was taken to the Thomas Clarke Farm where he lingered for nine days before dying.

At Trenton, Cornwallis found Washington gone at daybreak and assumed he had retired to Bordentown. At 8.00am he was surprised by reports of cannon fire to the east. It was only then did he realize Washington had given him the slip. He immediately ordered the British Guards to lead the army back toward Princeton. Brigadier-General Leslie, deployed at Maidenhead with the 2nd Brigade, also heard the exchange of cannon fire between Mawhood and Mercer. Although he had orders to march to Trenton he sent his men toward Princeton to assist Mawhood. At 10.00am the leading detachment of light cavalry and infantry found the Stony Brook Bridge destroyed and Potter's infantry, supported by Forrest's artillery barring any advance. The British immediately searched out fords along the creek and rushed across, overwhelming the American defenders and capturing Col. Potter. Leslie moved his brigade over Stony Brook but was unsure how large a force he faced and when American militia fired a British cannon inadvertently in one of the abandoned redoubts Leslie decided to wait for events to develop.

Washington entered Princeton about 9.00am and found Sullivan's men engaged in systematic looting, replacing their worn-out blankets with new British versions and loading flour into wagons. At approximately 10.00am Washington received reports of Leslie's approach and responded by putting an end to the looting and ordered Sullivan to collect his men. Supplies and arms were collected, including three brass 6-pdr guns abandoned by the British. A shortage of horses would not allow the guns to be removed but Major Thomas Proctor took advantage of the situation to trade his iron 3-pdr gun for one brass 6-pdr. By noon Sullivan's men were marching, followed by Greene's Division and Cadwalader and Mercer's brigades, which had remained outside Princeton, as Washington ordered his army to Kingston.

Alexander Hamilton's New York Company played a major role in the American retreat through New Jersey, the Hessian defeat at Trenton and the capture of Princeton. Hamilton's military career extended throughout the war, including playing an active role in the British defeat at Yorktown in 1781.

Restored room in the Thomas Clarke House in which Brig. Gen. Hugh Mercer was taken after the battle and where he died nine days later. Mercer had been wounded in the early phases of the battle while trying to rally his men near the William Clarke House. After falling from his horse he was surrounded by British troops and bayoneted after refusing to surrender. (Author's collection)

After confirming that the Americans were marching eastward out of Princeton, Leslie's Brigade moved into the village just after noon. Although the head of Cornwallis's column followed Leslie, his men were strung out along the road to Maidenhead and it wasn't until 4.00pm that they all reached Princeton. A small detachment of British light dragoons and light infantry were sent after the American column. Moulder's Company was ordered to slow the British pursuit with orders to abandon the guns should it prove necessary. Moulder's men deployed and initially scattered their pursuers. The British light infantry kept up a steady fire as Moulder's men tried to move the guns away and the British cavalry seemed ready to run down the American artillery. However, Captain Morris, with 22 men of the Philadelphia Light Horse, deployed across the road and discouraged the smaller group of British cavalry from charging, allowing Moulder to withdraw his guns.

At Kingston the Americans destroyed the bridge over Millstone Creek and Washington once again considered his options. Holding an impromptu council on horseback with his staff Washington was tempted by the siren call of New Brunswick, 18 miles distant. At New Brunswick he could replenish his army and secure weapons and ammunition. More importantly the loss of New Brunswick would further shake British resolve. Washington also considered the condition of his army. The men were exhausted from the fighting at Trenton, the midnight march, and the battles at the Clarke farms and Princeton. Now they were marching again with no real rest. Cornwallis was on his heels and he had no idea whether or not Howe had sent additional troops to New Brunswick. Someone suggested sending Sullivan's men, who were the least tired, to New Brunswick. Washington, who understood the danger of dividing his army in the face of the enemy, rejected the idea.

Reluctantly but prudently Washington selected the road that led to Somerset Court House and beyond to Morristown. The Americans marched through the late afternoon and reached Somerset in the evening. The weather, which had been mild, turned cold again and the men dropped wherever they could for rest.

On the morning of January 4 Washington and his men continued their march, reaching Bound Brook, where Washington looked wistfully once again toward New Brunswick. The continued sufferings of the army quickly resolved the issue and Washington marched six miles, crossed the Raritan River and continued another 10 miles to Pluckemin, where he stopped for two days to allow stragglers to catch up. On January 7 Washington established his headquarters at Morristown.

At the same time Cornwallis harbored no illusions about pursuing Washington. The safety of New Brunswick was paramount and Cornwallis pushed his men beyond Kingston, reaching New Brunswick at 6.00am on January 4. Still unsure of Washington's intentions Cornwallis deployed his men in defensive positions around New Brunswick until later in the day when it became clear the Americans were no immediate threat. The 10 critical days were over.

AFTERMATH

Although Washington had retired from the battlefield the fighting in the countryside continued. American militia attacked British forage details and patrols daily. On January 6 Howe ordered the British to abandon Elizabethtown and retire to Amboy. The militia harassed the British and Hessian troops as they retreated, capturing 100 prisoners and portions of the baggage train. Amboy proved no safe haven and the British were under constant pressure from the militia. Brigadier-General Knox wrote his wife "The enemy was within nineteen miles of Philadelphia, they are now sixty miles. We have driven them from almost the whole of West Jersey. The panic is still kept up …"

Throughout the winter Washington sent small detachments of Continentals to work with the militia to harass the British. From January through March large detachments of British and Hessians fought a series of running battles with American militia, supported by the few Continental units at Washington's disposal.

As British garrisons withdrew, the New Jersey loyalists were subjected to retribution by their Whig neighbors. Whether the loyalists abandoned their homes to seek relative safety in New York or once again swore allegiance to the American Congress, the resurgence of the militia doomed the Howes' strategy of reconciliation.

The British reaction to Trenton and Princeton was to try to minimize the Hessian defeat at Trenton, heap all the blame on the deceased Col. Rall, ignore their failure at Assunpink Creek and rewrite the history of their defeat at Princeton. Scorn was directed at the Hessians, despite their defense that Mawhood's Brigade had fared no better at Princeton than the Hessians did at Trenton. General Howe made no mention of the battle of Princeton other than to praise Lt. Col. Mawhood and the 17th Foot, and British newspapers reported Princeton as a British victory that cost the Americans 400 casualties. The general silence, on both sides, surrounding the battle of Assunpink Creek continues to this day.

In early March 1777, Lord George Germain unwittingly summed up the impact of the campaigns of Trenton and Princeton when he wrote to the Howe brothers, "I trust … that the unexpected success of the rebels will not so far elate them as to prevent them from seeing the real horrors of their situation and tempt them to disdain to sue for pardon."

A close examination of the retreat across New Jersey and the battles of Trenton and Princeton challenge two commonly held presumptions. The first is that the Howe brothers were complicit in a lackadaisical pursuit of Washington's retreating army and allowed it to escape for political reasons.

While the pursuit did suffer from moments of inertia, it can be explained in several ways. Howe's original intention was only to establish a strong foothold in New Jersey, not to pursue Washington across the entire state. Cornwallis was hampered by a series of shifting territorial objectives, marching in fits and starts as Howe revised his overall objectives several times. Cornwallis was also limited by his ever-lengthening supply lines. Most importantly, despite the legitimate criticism that he vacillated in joining Washington largely due to his own ambition, Charles Lee added to the discomfort of both Cornwallis and Howe by remaining elusive. Given the military stature afforded him by the British and commanding a force of 7,000 men, Howe and Cornwallis could only advance cautiously and always with an eye on their exposed right flank. If Lee had marched immediately at Washington's first request, with these combined forces Washington may have felt either emboldened enough to offer battle at New Brunswick or Princeton with uncertain prospects. Rather than put Washington in peril Lee's insubordination may well have convinced Washington that resistance was futile and delayed Cornwallis enough to ensure his escape.

The second myth is that Washington was somehow a mediocre strategist and battlefield commander. Although Washington was outgeneraled during the New York campaign and then again in 1777 during the Philadelphia campaign, his actions in December 1776 and January 1777 suggest a superior military mind.

Timing was everything and events that seemed to have upset his plan worked in Washington's favor. The storm of the evening of December 25, while precluding Cadwalader and Ewing from crossing, also kept the Hessians inside and their patrols from discovering Washington's crossing. At Princeton, the delay in crossing Quaker Bridge resulted in Mawhood with two regiments being separated from the one regiment left in Princeton. If Mercer had marched directly to the Stony Brook Bridge, Mawhood would have seen him and retired to Princeton. With his full command to defend Princeton the outcome of Washington's attack might have been very different.

The 10 days of the Trenton and Princeton campaign included three major engagements, one of which, the battle of Assunpink Creek, has been diminished in its importance. If we assume the actions on January 2, culminating with the assaults on the Assunpink Bridge, are part of a single action then the 500 plus casualties the British incurred represent a major engagement, on a par with Brandywine, Germantown and Monmouth.

At a dinner after his surrender at Yorktown in 1781 Cornwallis paid tribute to Washington's conduct of the Trenton and Princeton campaign. Responding to a toast Cornwallis offered that, "When the illustrious part that your Excellency has borne in this long and arduous contest becomes a matter of history fame will gather your brightest laurels rather from the banks of the Delaware than from those of the Chesapeake."

THE BATTLEFIELDS TODAY

Dedicated in 1922 by President Warren G. Harding, the Princeton Battle Monument is located in Princeton, New Jersey. The Monument commemorates the American victory and depicts Gen. George Washington leading American troops, and the death of Brig. Gen. Hugh Mercer. (Author's collection)

OPPOSITE
This monument to Gen. George Washington, erected in 1916 by the Patriot Order of Sons of America of Pennsylvania, is located at the Washington Crossing Park, Pennsylvania. The monument commemorates the point at which the American Army crossed the Delaware River. (Author's collection)

The battlefields of Trenton and Princeton provide a stark contrast for those interested in the battles. The landscape of the battlefield at Trenton has been dramatically altered as a result of 200 years of development and redevelopment. King (Warren) and Queen (Broad) streets continue to provide a dominant view from the deployment of the American artillery into town. The 150ft-tall Battle Monument is located at the head of King and Queen streets where the American artillery deployed. Throughout downtown Trenton there are plaques commemorating the location of buildings that figured in the battle. Of particular interest is the Old Barracks, still preserved and open as a visitor center and museum.

Subsequent development has dramatically altered the Assunpink Creek battlefield. The significant change in elevation along the south bank of the creek has been largely erased. Although the Douglass House, where Washington held his council of war on January 2 exists, it has been moved from its original location.

The Washington Crossing Historic Park in Pennsylvania provides two sites, reflecting the dispersed dispositions of Washington's Army. The McKonkey's Ferry site includes the McKonkey Ferry Inn and associated Visitors Center and Durham Boat House. Approximately three-and-a-half miles up the Delaware is the Thompson-Neely House, which functioned as Lord Sterling's headquarters and as a hospital.

On the New Jersey side of the Delaware the Washington Crossing State Park includes the Johnson Ferryhouse, which provided shelter to Gen. Washington and his staff during the crossing. The Swan Foundation's National Museum of the American Revolution, located in the Park, includes a museum with an extensive collection of arms and uniforms.

The Princeton Battlefield is centered around the Thomas Clarke Farm. One section of the Clarke Farmhouse has been devoted to a museum with displays of arms and artifacts from the battlefield. The other section of the house includes a restored kitchen and the bedroom in which Brig. Gen. Mercer died. A short walk from the Clarke Farm is the Quaker Meeting House and the Ionic Colonnade, which includes the graves of soldiers who died in the battle.

In Princeton, Nassau Hall on the campus of Princeton University is open to visitors. At the corner of Stockton Road and Nassau Street is the Princeton Battlefield Monument, dedicated in 1922.

BIBLIOGRAPHY

Bill, Alfred Hoyt, *The Campaign of Princeton 1776–77*, Princeton University Press: Princeton, NJ, 1948

Buchanan, John, *The Road to Valley Forge*, John Wiley and Sons: New York, 2004

Butcher, H. Borton, *The Battle of Trenton*, Princeton University Press: Princeton, NJ, 1934

Chadwick, Bruce, *The First American Army*, Sourcebooks Inc: Naperville, IL, 2005

Chidsey, Donald Barr, *The Tide Turns*, Crown Publishers: New York, 1966

Collins, Varnum Lansing, *A Brief Narrative of the Ravages of the British and Hessians at Princeton in 1776–77*, Drunthwacket Foundation: Princeton, NJ, 1999

Drake, Samuel Adams, *The Campaign of Trenton, 1776–77*, Scholars Bookshelf: Cranbury, NJ, 1895

Dwyer, William M., *The Day is Ours*, Viking Press: New York, 1983

Ferling, John, *Almost a Miracle*, Oxford University Press: New York, 2007

Fischer, David Hackett, *Washington's Crossing*, Oxford University Press: New York, 2004

Golway, Terry, *Washington's General*, Henry Holt and Company: New York, 2006

Headley, J.T., *Washington and His Generals*, Scribners: New York, 1857

Katcher, Phillip, *Encyclopedia of British, Provincial and German Army Units, 1775–1783*, Stackpole Books: Mechanicsburg, PA, 1973

Katcher, Phillip, *Armies of the American Wars 1753–1815*, Hastings House: New York, 1975

Katcher, Phillip, *Uniforms of the Continental Army*, George Shumway: New York, 1981

Ketchum, Richard M., *The Winter Soldiers*, Henry Holt: New York, 1973

Kwasny, Mark V., *Washington's Partisan War*, Kent State Press: Kent, OH, 1996

Lefkowitz, Arthur S., *The Long Retreat*, Rutgers University Press: New Brunswick, NJ, 1999

Lengel, Edward G., *General George Washington*, Random House: New York, 2005

Marshall, Douglas W. and Howard H. Peckham, *Campaigns of the American Revolution*, University of Michigan Press: Ann Arbor, MI, 1976

McCullough, David, *1776*, Simon and Schuster: New York, 2005

Mollo and McGregor, *Uniforms of the American Revolution*, Macmillan Publishing: New York, 1975

Pancake, John S., *1777 The Year of the Hangman*, University of Alabama Press: Tuscaloosa, AL, 1977

Patterson, Benton Rain, *Washington and Cornwallis*, Taylor Trade Publishing: New York, 2004

Roswurm, Steven, *Arms, Country and Class*, Rutgers University Press: New Brunswick, NJ, 1987

Schecter, Barnet, *The Battle for New York*, Walker and Company: New York, 2002

Seymour, William, *The Price of Folly*, Brassey's: London, 1995

Smith, Samuel Stelle, *Battle of Trenton*, Phillip Freneau Press: Monmouth Beach, NJ, 1965

Smith, Samuel Stelle, *The Battle of Princeton*, Phillip Freneau Press: Monmouth Beach, NJ, 1967

Stephenson, Michael, *Patriot Battles*, Harper Collins: New York, 2007

Stryker, William S., *The Battles of Trenton and Princeton*, Old Barracks Association: Trenton, NJ, 2001

Thane, Elswyth, *The Fighting Quaker*, Aeonian Press: Mattituck, NY, 1977

Thompson, Ray, *Washington Along the Delaware*, Bicentennial Press, 1970

Troiani, Don, *Soldiers of the American Revolution*, Stackpole: Mechanicsburg, PA, 2007

Urban, Mark, *Fusiliers*, Walker Publishing: New York, 2007

Woodhull, Alfred A., *The Battle of Princeton*, W. C. Sinclair: Princeton, NJ, 1913

Washington and His Generals, Claxton, Remsen and Haffelfinger: New York, 1875

Wright, Robert K., *The Continental Army*, United States Army Center of Military History, 1989

INDEX

References to illustrations are shown in **bold**. Subheadings are arranged in page number order.